WHY

THE S

RETAIL MAVERICK
AND
COURTS

WHY NOT?

THE **STORY** OF A **RETAIL MAVERICK** AND **COURTS**

TERRY O'CONNOR O.B.E.

Marshall Cavendish Editions

© 2013 Marshall Cavendish International (Asia) Private Limited

Photographs by Courts Asia Limited, cover art and design by Benson Tan

Published by Marshall Cavendish Editions
An imprint of Marshall Cavendish International
1 New Industrial Road, Singapore 536196

All rights reserved

No part of this publication may be reproduced, stored in a retrieval system or transmitted, in any form or by any means, electronic, mechanical, photocopying, recording or otherwise, without the prior permission of the copyright owner. Requests for permission should be addressed to the Publisher, Marshall Cavendish International (Asia) Private Limited, 1 New Industrial Road, Singapore 536196. Tel: (65) 6213 9300, fax: (65) 6285 4871. E-mail: genref@sg.marshallcavendish.com. Website: www.marshallcavendish.com/genref

The publisher makes no representation or warranties with respect to the contents of this book, and specifically disclaims any implied warranties or merchantability or fitness for any particular purpose, and shall in no event be liable for any loss of profit or any other commercial damage, including but not limited to special, incidental, consequential, or other damages.

Other Marshall Cavendish Offices:
Marshall Cavendish Corporation. 99 White Plains Road, Tarrytown NY 10591-9001, USA • Marshall Cavendish International (Thailand) Co Ltd. 253 Asoke, 12th Flr, Sukhumvit 21 Road, Klongtoey Nua, Wattana, Bangkok 10110, Thailand • Marshall Cavendish (Malaysia) Sdn Bhd, Times Subang, Lot 46, Subang Hi-Tech Industrial Park, Batu Tiga, 40000 Shah Alam, Selangor Darul Ehsan, Malaysia.

Marshall Cavendish is a trademark of Times Publishing Limited

National Library Board, Singapore Cataloguing-in-Publication Data
O'Connor, Terry, OBE
Why Not? : The Story of a Retail Maverick and Courts / Terry O'Connor, OBE. — Singapore : Marshall Cavendish Editions, 2013.
      pages . cm.
ISBN : 978-981-4328-72-2 (paperback)

1. O'Connor, Terry, OBE. 2. Courts (Firm) — History 3. Businessmen — Great Britain — Biography I. Title.

HC102.5
338.092 — dc23   OCN839182356

Printed by Markono Print Media Pte Ltd

Dedication

I hope this book sparks the dreams of
aspiring executives or young leaders
to break through a setback,
challenge a restraining norm
and achieve their full potential.

Yet, in the bluntest sense, it's a record—
for my wife, Janice,
my kids, Daniel and Jennifer,
my amazing friends, my 'book team'
and my YPO Forum—
who all gave me the courage to finish the job.

*All proceeds of this book will go to
the 'Make-a-Wish' foundation.*

Contents

Introduction		9
Chapter 1:	**Terry Across the Mersey**	19
Chapter 2:	**Baptism by Fire: Retail Beginnings**	36
Chapter 3:	**The Incongruities of a Family-Run Global Business**	60
Chapter 4:	**Singapore Fling**	81
Chapter 5:	**Creating a Counter Culture**	96
Chapter 6:	**The Non-Linear Path to the Top**	107
Chapter 7:	**Taking Charge**	137
Chapter 8:	**Holding Things Together by Reaching Out**	163
Chapter 9:	**Who Needs a Head Office Anyway?**	175
Chapter 10:	**Putting the House in Order**	193
Chapter 11:	**Full Steam Ahead**	207
Chapter 12:	**Blueprint 2.0**	219
Chapter 13:	**Going Public**	228
Chapter 14:	**Thinking Big[ger]**	237
About the Author		243

Introduction

Even after more than two decades, I am still amazed at the unlikelihood that I, a born-and-bred Scouser, am running one of Singapore's top retail chains. (A 'Scouser' is a resident of Liverpool, and Scouse is the dialect of English spoken in Liverpool.) It's as unlikely as the fact that the stores I run—a combination consumer electronics and home lifestyle retailer—began life as a dowdy furniture shop in Canterbury, England in 1850.

Or, perhaps it's not so unlikely. But both I and the company I run, Courts Asia Limited, exemplify the kind of success that can be achieved by daring to cross boundaries, grab improbable opportunities, and build tight links with foreign communities. Who says you can't?

Consider, for example, the remarkable transformation of Courts. When Albert Court opened a small, family-run furniture shop in Canterbury, England in 1850, he probably had no ambitions to turn it into a global brand that, at its peak, would operate in 22 countries and earn the UK's "International Retailer of the Year" (according to *Retail Week* in 1997). Nor could he have imagined the buzz of electronics that greets Courts' customers when they walk into a store.

Indeed, it wasn't until the Cohen family acquired the business in the 1940s that the Courts Group began expanding its global footprint. The Cohens had a strong background in home furnishings, and they used their knowledge of the market to expand in England. In the late 1950s, they ventured overseas with the unlikely (yet visionary) choice of setting up in the Caribbean island of Jamaica. Ironically, this turned out to be a runaway success story that led to further expansion in the region. I might even say that the founding fathers of this international drive were decades ahead of their time when viewed in the context of today's globalised business!

Courts' expansion to international markets veered to the Eastern Hemisphere beginning in the late 1960s, with entry into Australia, Hong Kong, Fiji, Papua New Guinea, Singapore, Malaysia, Mauritius, Indonesia and Madagascar, and further expansion in the West Indies. By the 1990s, Courts operated stores in some of the world's most exotic resort destinations, including Barbados, Antigua and Bali.

By the early 1990s, after exits from Australia and Hong Kong and subsequent entry into Malaysia (1987) and Indonesia (1994), Courts' business balanced on three centres of gravity: the UK, Southeast Asia and the Caribbean. The latter two were successful, market-leading businesses. But the UK home market was increasingly wavering under expensive high-street rents and costs associated with generous benefits and accumulation of company assets, such as cars.

In a 2001 review by the then-incoming group chairman, the managing directors of the top six overseas countries were recalled to London to give their views on the future of the Courts Group. The overwhelming feedback was to close the UK retail business and establish a small corporate centre to give guidance and support to overseas territories. In contast to stores such as Ikea and Furniture Village, the UK business had been slow to adopt large-format 'out of town' retail; nor had it harnessed the consumer electronics wave (unlike its overseas subsidiaries), and was, at best, fifth in the UK furniture market standings. In short, Courts had lost touch with its customers.

The executive management team was by this time comprised of family members who were in many cases ill-equipped for the scale and complexity of the roles they held.

What's more, many bright managers who were brought in were neutralised by organisational or family politics and disempowered. Even the most successful executives in the Courts overseas network failed when given UK roles—not due to lack of ability, but rather an inability to execute in a tight family-controlled environment.

The clear solution, at least for the 'group of six', was to sell or close the UK base and focus on the international business—in particular, South America and Southeast Asia, which were both well placed to take advantage of the growth in their emerging retail economies.

This advice was well received by the chairman, but unequivocally rejected by the family-controlled board of directors.

Ultimately, all 88 Courts stores in the UK were closed in 2004 by KPMG, the administrator hired by a consortium of banks to handle the group's central debt, which had ballooned to £315 million. Whilst having very successful overseas subsidiaries that were generally number one or number two in their respective markets, Courts occupied a relatively low-end in the UK furniture retail sector and had struggled with relatively low market power for many years. In spite of this, it had continued to expand, and continued to build debt.

One of the reasons Courts' branches overseas began outperforming Courts UK was their ability to adapt to the changing consumer tastes of emerging markets, such as interest in lively branding, big-box retailing, and electronics. Unlike in their parent company, frequent management changes in these overseas operations helped to keep the brand fresh. Many of Courts' companies overseas also operated a strong consumer finance business, while Courts UK had sold its consumer finance business in the 1980s.

The upshot was disastrous for Courts PLC. By November 2004, after 154 years of trading, the Courts parent company was collapsing.

And yet, here in Singapore, business was steady—held together by a strong management team *and* the overwhelming support of the Singaporean community. In fact, Courts UK's administration allowed a newly empowered Asian subsidiary, Courts Singapore, to consolidate Asian operations and achieve remarkable growth.

While there were no significant financial linkages between our Singapore subsidiary and the UK parent, and our business was not in administration, perception can have a powerful effect. We worried about public reaction to our parent's difficulties. To avoid a crisis of confidence, we developed a precise communication strategy to reassure our business partners, our customers and the community at large, especially the media. And it worked. When Courts UK finally went under in 2004, headlines in Singapore read simply: "Courts Singapore unaffected despite parent's woes"

The lesson here was the importance of relationships—the trust our staff placed in me and our team; Courts' openness to the media, which ensured the story was told fairly and accurately; and the overwhelming support of trade partners who reviewed our independent balance sheets and maintained their trust in us.

Over the following weeks towards the end of the year, our fears subsided and a sense of independence and opportunity kicked in. My team had one overriding aim: to find new ownership that would ensure our future and, at the same time, to try to unify the Southeast Asian businesses, which comprised two separately listed entities in Singapore and Malaysia.

We sensed a brand headquartered in London for 154 years could be succeeded by a youthful Asia-based entity, one that had bigger and bolder plans for Asia, and with consumer electronics as its core offering. With large-format stores and a more diverse leadership, could we make a transition from subsidiary to HQ? Could we persuade the UK administrator to keep the Asia business together? Could a Singapore HQ become a reality? While the scenario was fraught with uncertainty, we also saw it to be full of possibilities, and felt that the opportunity to succeed was there for the taking.

We would ultimately spend three years in the shop window as the Courts group was parcelled up worldwide, but achieving our dream through unshakeable belief would be possible in spite of many obstacles as long as we focused on becoming the new headquarters for Courts.

Our destiny would be further complicated by the mixed fortunes of Southeast Asia during the administration years. Whilst the Singapore business would continue to prosper, the subsidiary companies in Malaysia, Indonesia and Thailand were faring less well—a significant issue when those three markets were home to 143 stores compared to the 10 in Singapore!

After a few false starts with potential suitors, we agreed to a deal in May 2007 with a consortium led by Baring Private Equity Asia (BPEA). The consortium agreed to buy both Courts Singapore and Courts M Berhad (Malaysia), and set in motion the merger of the two entities, thus helping us to create the kind of company that I had long envisioned for Courts.

I came to Singapore in 1993 as a Buying Director. Young (just 25 years old) and ambitious, I had already been working full-time for eight years, and married for four. In another example of finding opportunity in unlikely places, I should mention that I met my wife, Janice, at a fish-and-chips shop that I frequented in Liverpool. She was helping her family—recent immigrants from Hong Kong—run the business.

Though at the time I had my eyes set on the goal of one day running a business, I could hardly have imagined that almost two decades later the 160-year-old Courts brand would have disappeared from the UK marketplace, reinvented itself as one of Southeast Asia's retail giants, and that I would be contemplating the future as a financially independent retail maverick.

This is not your standard rags-to-riches autobiography. I'm only 45, after all, and my life lacks fame and glamour. Nor is it a pure-play academic retail book. It is also not merely about corporate re-invention. There are plenty of books out there describing the making of multimillion-dollar businesses and the leaders that build them. But how much money I make—or how much Courts makes—doesn't get to the heart of the story.

The heart of the story is the cultivation of attitude, ethics and vision (or, as my first corporate mentor likes to say, Knowledge, Ability and Commitment), and how far these traits can take you as long as you hold on in the toughest of times. It's about pushing boundaries, surviving, and ultimately thriving—seeing opportunity in crisis. Ultimately it's a story that hopefully inspires, in some small way, executives and to think through the possibilities of *how to make the best* of humble backgrounds, corporate roadblocks, market turbulence or other setbacks.

I hope to show that somewhere in between the traditional toe-the-line, command-and-control way of moving up an organisation and today's Gen Y touchy, feely, bruise easily attitude, there's a middle ground that says you still need to work hard, you still need to do the right things, but you can actually dare to be different, you can challenge the norm. You can be a little bit of a maverick while taking controlled, intelligent risks.

If nothing else, I hope it inspires you to think about what's next for you personally as an executive, for your company, or for your industry, and that it serves as part of the process that transports you there through your greatest personal asset—your attitude.

It isn't possible to accumulate enough clear-minded observations across the first half of one's career to produce an interesting read, let alone find the time to write a book without the support of a loving family—one that integrates work, life and play in a way that means sacrifices are rarely necessary on any one component. So I say to my family: thank you.

Terry O'Connor (June 2013)

CHAPTER 1
Terry Across the Mersey

When faced with adversity at an early age, you learn to use internal resources to get what you need, whether it's money, material goods, or mentors. Finding bright spots in dark places is part luck and part persistence.

To understand how unlikely it is that I have helped create one of Singapore's—and now, Southeast Asia's—leading retailers, you have to consider where I came from. I spent my childhood in an area of Liverpool known as Anfield. Born in 1968 in Birkenhead, which is across the river Mersey from Liverpool, I moved to Liverpool proper when I was three. Our family lived in public housing on July Road—just a stone's throw from Liverpool's now famous football ground, which naturally makes me a lifelong Liverpool Football Club fan. We had an old, red brick three-bedroom Council house with a brick outhouse for a toilet. Nearby there was a railway track that we called 'Black Hills' because of its black, sooty embankment that we used to play on. At the end of the street were three well-frequented pubs. It was a relatively poor part of the city, but not as rough as some of the neighbourhoods we would end up in a few years later.

By most measures, my childhood was less than idyllic. My dad—a hard-drinking Irishman—was in and out of work most of the time. My mum was a meek and soft lady, although she was consistently thoughtful. She always remembered birthdays—not just mine, but also those of my uncles, aunts, cousins and distant cousins. She always made sure that I was groomed and getting to school, though she didn't seem to be aware of what I was *doing* at school. Even when I quit school at 17, I don't remember her having much of a reaction. She often complained of illnesses, though the doctors could never pinpoint a problem.

Perhaps my mum's attitude was indicative of a broader malaise related to her relationship with my dad. To this day, I can't remember more than a few times that we spent time together as a family. Not voluntarily, at least. My dad made sure to attend formal family events—things like weddings and funerals. But our immediate family didn't go out together, first, because we didn't have the money, and second, because my mum and dad rarely got along, and even eventually divorced.

This is not to say that they didn't look after me and my brother Paul, who was born in 1976. Dad would walk a few miles to pick up his benefit cheque so that he could save the bus fare and have some spare change to give to us to use as pocket money. I also recall a particular bright spot early on, when he had a job for a while with Barker and Dobson, a local sweet manufacturer, and he would bring home sweets that we otherwise couldn't have afforded to buy.

When I was seven, our family situation took a turn for the worse. My father, who was frustrated with being jobless, ran off to Ireland and we didn't hear from him for about five or six weeks. Eventually he made contact and we learned that he was with his sister and had found a job working at the Edenvale yogurt factory. We followed him there several months later, which we quickly discovered was a bad decision.

First off, I went from a run-of-the-mill public primary school in Liverpool to an Irish school called De La Salle that was run by a Christian brotherhood. There was no such thing as a leather strap in Liverpool, but I can tell you from experience that at De La Salle, if you didn't do your homework, you'd get a whacking. I remember coming home one day and telling my aunt Kay that I had been strapped. She asked why, and when I said it was because I didn't do my homework, she said, "It bloody serves you right." So there wasn't much sympathy there—and not much about the whole situation in general to leave any fond memories of Ireland.

There was not much about the situation to leave any fond memories of Ireland.

The cost of living was quite high in Ireland, even for little luxuries. I distinctly remember being very upset that Christmas, in 1976, because I didn't have any money to buy presents for anyone. We were also living in my aunt's house, with everyone packed in on top of each other. At the time, my brother was just a few months old, which added to the hectic feel in the household. After a year, the family decided to return to Liverpool for a better life. My mum, brother and I went first, with my dad agreeing to follow when we found a place to stay. The trouble was that the situation in Liverpool wasn't much better.

When we first returned, we lived in what can only be described as a sheltered accommodation before moving in with my uncle Peter, my mum's brother, for a while. Eventually, my mum found a public housing flat to rent in a neighbourhood called Croxteth, where my dad joined us six months later. It wasn't the greatest part of town, and my dad's joining us didn't work out, but this was a place where I found some stability during my childhood.

To give you an idea of the neighbourhood, Croxteth later laid claim to the dubious honour of being the drug capital of Liverpool. Somehow, our street must have been an oasis—it was near Croxteth Country Park, one of the most beautiful parks in the north of England, and the lord mayor of Liverpool lived on our street. But if you walked the other direction, you quickly got into some estates that were quite rough. I recall that a nearby pub called The Dog and Gun had a particularly bad reputation.

But as in Liverpool, I managed to meet some great lads in Croxteth with whom I'm still close today. We met kicking a ball against a wall in the street, and we ended up forming this close-knit group of four mates who hung out together. I think we were probably the only guys in the whole area who didn't smoke or do drugs or all that. We still chased girls and all the usual boy stuff as we got older, but stayed away from the more unsavoury things happening around us.

My performance in primary school was something of a bright spot in my early years, as I was generally number one or number two out of about 80 kids in my year. At the age of 11, I was awarded a scholarship for St Edwards College, a grammar school that normally would be fee-paying. I distinctly remember saying to my dad that I didn't care for the 'posh school' and wanted to go to the other, normal school where my mates were going. This didn't go over particularly well, and I ultimately and emphatically lost that argument.

That was also around the same time that my parents divorced and my father moved out. I didn't have much of a reaction to the breakup for about a year, and whether that was from not really understanding the implications, or not wanting to confront the reality, I'm not sure. I think that, because they'd separated on numerous occasions before this, I initially thought that this was just another temporary split. But by the time I was 13 or 14, I came to realise that it was permanent, and, though saddened by it, that it was actually better for both of them.

My father's departure removed an element of discipline from my life. He had always been quite strict—not in the academic sense, but in overseeing my behaviour. He would be the one hanging out the window telling me to get in the house when it was curfew time, or he would come down to the fields to call me home if I was playing football. And while my father was not a very educated man, he was certainly pro-education, which had helped to keep me focused on school.

My grades went to pieces.

But after the move to St Edwards College, and the divorce, I went from being right at the top of my class every year to being an average student. I no longer stood out as the bright one in class, and this contributed to my feeling a bit depressed. I started to lose interest in school and began playing football every night with my friends rather than studying. Predictably, my grades went to pieces.

Around this time I also began attending a prayer group at school. At the meetings, I often strummed a guitar (badly!) while singing church songs. The students running the group were slightly older than I, and I remember admiring them for their respect for moral values and desire to share these values with others. Although I stopped actively pursuing religious interests after a few years, I believe this period influenced my subsequent development. I had found something positive to pursue during a difficult time. I had no musical experience, I was significantly younger than the other group members, but I didn't let that deter me from joining. And I was welcomed with enthusiasm. If nothing else, I know it took some of the edge off of my sometimes-rough childhood.

A CAMPING TRIP FOR COMMUNITY BUILDING—A GLIMPSE AT THE POWER OF CHARITY

It was around this time—I was around 13 years old —that I met my uncle John, my mother's brother, while visiting my sick grandmother. I didn't know it, but this meeting marked an important turning point in my life, as John's mentorship directed me toward a path of entrepreneurialism and public service.

During our visit, he asked me if I had ever done any camping. I said yes, which was technically true, although the only camping I'd ever done was when my mates and I had snuck away for the weekend and pitched a tent on a mountainside in Wales without telling our parents (we got into serious trouble for that!). But he took my answer at face value, and suggested that I join him for a holiday that summer.

What I didn't realise at the time was that he and my aunt ran a charity called the Northwest Handicapped Children's Society. They ran a holiday programme for handicapped kids in a school, and another summer camp for underprivileged kids. Now I wasn't all that refined myself, but I was assigned to be the helper at the camp, and it turned out that I relished my position. I also thrived amidst the close-knit family of Uncle John and his five children, which provided a welcome contrast to mine. I ended up helping at the summer camp every year, and it became something I looked forward to each time.

Looking back, I can see that around this time a sense of responsibility started to kick in. Besides the experience at the camp, there were a number of other factors that pushed me over the edge from carefree child to a somewhat more mature youth. One was my mother, who was a single parent and didn't have much money. Another was my school, St Edwards College, which was pretty good at instilling values. And there was Uncle John, who started to provide some more oversight and also became interested in how I was doing academically.

Uncle John was the one who suggested that instead of playing football and hanging out with my mates over the holidays, I should come and stay at his place, which was about 30 miles away. I took him up on this offer, and he was a good influence. As a result, I spent many of my holidays over the next two years at Uncle John's house in the countryside. It was a quiet place with very few opportunities for getting into trouble. With Uncle John showing interest in my academics and some productive holidays, my studies picked up to the point where I actually did pass some GCSEs; enough to carry me through to do A Levels, which had been looking increasingly unlikely two years earlier.

And despite my grades, St Edwards was also a good environment for me. I was mixing with a completely different set of kids than I was used to. I considered many of them to be from quite rich families, although I later realised that they were just your average middle-class kids. My teachers were very supportive, and one in particular, a man named Sheedy, took an interest in how I was doing. He heard about my parents' divorce and took the time to drive me home one day after school to talk with my mom and understand the situation. Sheedy learnt that I played chess and encouraged me to join the chess club. As unlikely as it sounds, I ended up as the club captain and placed third in the Liverpool schools tournament in 1980, when I was 12 years old. It was my first taste of the highs that come from successful and challenging team environments.

FROM TOP OF THE CLASS TO DOOR-TO-DOOR SALES: UPWARDS, SIDEWAYS OR DOWNWARDS?

These schooldays proved quite a contrast to my weekends at this time. In an effort to spend quality time together, my father, who was working the slot machines at Wilkie's Pleasure Park and Indoor Fairground in New Brighton, got me a job taking tickets and working rides on the weekends. The pay and the hours were absolutely horrible, but it was a chance for me to see my dad during breaks. And it was a great way to chat up girls!

I worked at the fairground for a few years, and it piqued my interest in the working world. A number of my friends who were a year or two older than I, also played a part in this. By the time I was 15, many of these friends had already left school and entered the workforce.

It was not unusual, then, that when I was 16 and had completed my O Levels and was heading into summer vacation, I picked up the paper to look at the jobs column. I saw an ad for a door-to-door canvasser job at a company called Tudor Stone, which was selling exterior stone cladding and Weathertex siding for houses. I went down and had an interview in the afternoon. The sales manager

> **We were always in the middle of one financial crisis or another.**

A young Terry with his wife, Janice.

was called Billy Boare, and I remember joking with him about his name—I was sure it was a trade name, but he swore it was his real name. Maybe because of that, Billy took a liking to me and asked me when I could start.

I joined a team of mostly older sales guys, and we were tasked with going door-to-door across Liverpool, setting up leads for the regional sales director. We had a load of fun. Sometimes we would invent the script, throwing in a curveball to see if anyone would notice. I was treated like one of the older guys as well, so we'd stop at the pub and have a couple of beers after work.

Besides the camaraderie, what really pleased me was that I discovered that I was quite a good salesman. I became very good at building a rapport with the customers. I found that I could get on their good side by suggesting negotiation tactics for when the sales director would visit. My pride and joy was a stretch of four houses in a row on one street where I'd set up deals. This was pretty much unheard of, and the sales director was hugely impressed as well.

With these kinds of successes, I was earning close to £100 a week, which added up to a few thousand pounds by the end of the summer. This was in the early 1980s and I was 16, so it was a substantial amount of money. I used it to buy a hi-fi system and a music collection, and I was also helping out my mum with money. She was on welfare benefits, and we were always in the middle of one financial crisis or another, so it felt good to be able to help her out.

WHO SAYS YOU CAN'T DROP OUT OF SCHOOL AND SUCCEED?

I returned to school the next autumn with a different mindset. It's difficult to explain, but I suppose it was the realisation that I could earn money and interact on an equal footing with people older than me. And so during that first term back, I enjoyed something of a different dimension in terms of dealing with the people around me. At the same time, I had this nagging idea of leaving school before completing my A Levels.

For a while I was able to put this thought aside, as I had opened a bank account and I had a good amount of money from the work I'd done over the summer. But

I slowly began to run out of cash and I realised I wasn't going to be able to support my mum as much as I had been. Quite frankly, I'd just gotten used to having a bit of money.

So in 1985 I made the decision to leave school, and mid-way through A Levels I just walked out. The teachers were horrified. And I have to admit that when the door of school closed behind me that day I was very emotional. I knew there were arguments against my leaving, but I had carefully thought it through. I wasn't going to have enough money to go to university, and there was in my mind a pretty clear need to start earning money sooner rather than later. I was adamant that this was the right decision.

I've never regretted my decision to leave. At the time, it was the right thing to do given my situation. I did, however, make a pledge to myself that I would return to education in some way, shape or form further down the road—just not right then.

I had been keeping up with the door-to-door sales job on weekends and in the evenings, but I knew that I didn't really fancy going back to hard selling. The novelty of pitching every house down a street had worn off a bit, and I thought it was time to try something new. So I took a look at the job market and quickly found a position with

Ocean Transport and Trading, one of the oldest shipping firms in Liverpool, as a shipping clerk.

The job involved mostly clerical work, and very quickly I was bored to distraction. At my first appraisal, I received feedback that I didn't appear to be engaged or working hard. My reply to this was to admit frankly that I was bored. I explained that I would often repeat tasks, such as writing memos, just to keep myself occupied.

To be fair, my boss handled this well, asking what it was that I wanted to do if this job wasn't interesting me. I explained that what I really wanted was to work in London or at least to go elsewhere or do something more exciting. He suggested that if I needed time off to look for another job or to take a punt around London, I should go and do it.

I took him up on this offer and made a few hopeful trips down to London, where I walked the streets looking for jobs, going to employment agencies and generally just poking my nose about. But I quickly realised that without an address in London, there was little hope of landing a job there. I also knew I didn't have enough money to get a place in London, so it was a bit of a catch-22 situation. With that, I struck London off my list for the time being and returned to Liverpool to continue my search there.

LESSON

My experience at Ocean Transport taught me early on a valuable lesson about work: **Do something that comes naturally.** It is worth taking the time to find work that interests you, that makes use of your skills and personality. For me, this was decidedly not a desk-bound job doing administrative work as a shipping clerk at Ocean Transport and Trading in Liverpool (thankfully, I figured this out quite quickly). I was fortunate to discover early on that some of my abilities—talking to people, negotiating, being quick with numbers—are a natural fit with the retail industry.

ALWAYS READ YOUR JOB OFFER LETTERS

Shortly thereafter, I saw an advert in the *Liverpool Echo* for a trainee buyer for a company called Colorvision. At the time Colorvision was a growing electrical chain with seven stores, and it seemed like as good an opportunity as any other, so I went for an interview with Cliff Proctor, the head of buying. He and I seemed to get on quite well, and he offered me a job after the second interview. Foolishly, I didn't actually ask about, let alone negotiate, the pay.

I guess I assumed that my wages would be higher since, in my mind, the wages at Ocean Transport and Trading were pretty meagre.

Rest assured that I've never made that mistake again: when I received my appointment letter, I realised the starting salary was £200 a year less than what I had been earning! Nonetheless, I still wanted the job and was bored where I was, so I bit the bullet and accepted. And so it was that in June 1986 at the age of 18, for the princely sum of £2,962 a year, I entered the retail business with Colorvision.

CHAPTER 2

Baptism by Fire: Retail Beginnings

A good mentor is one who can support you at the same time that they throw you into the deep end and force you to swim. They will push you to your limits and earn your respect, all the while teaching you how to stand up for your beliefs.

Joining Colorvision as a trainee buyer turned out to be a pivotal point in my career. Not only did it get me into the retail industry, it also introduced me to Neville Michaelson, Colorvision's chairman. Like my uncle John, Neville became one of the most important influences on my personal and professional development.

When I started at Colorvision, I was working under the guidance of Cliff Proctor. He showed me the ropes and we were getting on well. However, within a relatively short space of time, Cliff went on extended sick leave. Colorvision was small enough at the time that this meant I was suddenly getting much more face time with the chairman, Neville Michaelson. He was a seriously scary man—extremely aggressive and larger than life.

The chairman was a seriously scary man.

Neville was the kind of boss who would bound into the office and say, "Can you do this, this and this," assigning about two days worth of tasks. Then he'd bound in an hour later and ask, "Have you completed your assignments?" It wasn't that he was unreasonably demanding—he just wanted to remain on top of things. When I told him I was still finishing up some work that Cliff had asked me to do earlier, Neville replied, "Is Cliff the chairman? No, I'm the chairman, so what I want you to do takes priority."

He once pinned me to the wall while explaining that he didn't want me to be another 'yes man', and that I needed to think independently and tell him when he was wrong. While I understood the message, his

Neville Michaelson

delivery could be quite intimidating! Being new to the job, I was scared stiff of Neville.

When Cliff left due to illness, another executive named Mike Conboy was pulled in to manage buying. He had been on the property side of the business, working on store openings and the like, so buying wasn't really his area of expertise, although he was a skilled negotiator. Luckily, Mike and I clicked right away. He saw what I was doing and said it looked like I was pretty organised—he probably got this impression from the long lists I used to keep to stay on top of what I was doing and what needed to be done. I was also really enjoying the work, so I told him I thought I knew what I was doing. Mike admitted that he didn't really know anything about buying, so we agreed that I'd keep going with how I was handling the buying, and he would act like a shield between Neville and me. In any case, he sat directly opposite me, so he could stay plugged into what was going on, and I could always turn to him for help if I needed it. The result of all this was that after just a few months, I was thrust into a role of buying and negotiating deals that really made a difference to the company!

He didn't want me to be another 'yes man'.

HOW TO TAME A DEMANDING BOSS (PROCEED AT YOUR OWN RISK)

I think Neville had a discussion with Mike and asked why I was scared of him, to which Mike replied that maybe it was because he was the chairman and I was 18 years old. After that, my contact with Neville increased—I was asked to go into his office and change his price list and complete some commercial tasks. I'd try to get in and out of his office as quickly as possible, but every time I'd get to the door, Neville would invite me to sit down for a chat. I don't know if this was by design, or not, but looking back now, I have the feeling they had a clear plan to develop me. He saw in me a clean slate that he could mould into the kind of buyer he wanted for his company, rather than having to take on someone with experience who had already formed habits from working elsewhere. As you'll see below, I'm not the type of person who is easily moulded. But Neville's patient 'tough love' infected me, and today I am a better manager because of him.

At that time—around 1987—Colorvision had 12 stores and we seemed to be opening one or two new ones every month. And one day Neville called me into the boardroom together with his brother Bernard and a store manager called Ronnie Orr. He then proceeded to go absolutely ballistic on me. It turned out that Ronnie was opening a new store in Rochdale the following Saturday and that there was no stock for the store. Neville really launched into me on this one, accusing me of not doing my job and not organising the store for the opening. In response, I lost it.

"Well, are you finished?" I said. As you might guess, this got his attention and he bolted upright, looking shocked. I then went into a rant of my own: "You're the chairman, I'm an 18-year-old junior buyer. Cliff is sick and I'm holding this office together. And I've never met Ronnie, I don't even know who Ronnie Orr is, and I certainly didn't know we were opening a store in Rochdale. I haven't seen any store opening list, I haven't seen any formal plan, I'm not privy to any conversations you and your brother have, or you and the board have. All I can tell you is that if you communicate properly where we're opening, who we're hiring and what needs to be done, I will do what is required. But if you don't, I can't. So, I really think that you guys need to get your act together." And then I walked out.

I've just told the chairman where to shove it.

I walked downstairs to our main store, which was just below the offices, and I sat there. The store manager came over and asked if I was ok, as I was looking quite shaken. "I think I've just gotten sacked," was my reply. "I've just told the chairman where to shove it." Bear in mind that I was not consciously defying the chairman, I was simply standing up for what I thought was right for the company.

Then Bernard came down about 30 minutes later and told me Neville was very impressed, "You shouldn't do that too often, but your point was well-stated."

That was a huge turning point in our relationship. I obviously didn't want to be that impetuous all the time, but he obviously wanted me to stand my ground and speak my mind. From then on it became very much a father-son type relationship, and we still keep in contact today. I'll send him stuff now and then, like articles where I've referenced him, or things that I think may be of interest to him.

WHO SAYS A COMPANY CAN'T TRUST A 20-YEAR-OLD WITH MILLIONS?

In many ways, a lot of what Neville believed in and his entrepreneurial qualities are what I believe in. When I joined Colorvision, Neville was just introducing the Management Enterprise Network, which was a system whereby the store managers paid £10,000 for a 20 per cent profit share in their store. Neville saw it as a way to ensure that the store managers were there not just to manage an outlet and collect a salary, but had a real stake in the business and would do their best to grow sales and profits. He gave them a relatively free rein in how the stores were run, which made for some challenges in my work—it's much easier to deal with someone who is following clearly defined instructions than a bunch of profit-hungry entrepreneurs who want to negotiate their own deals and run things their own way!

This experience was invaluable, as **It was mind-blowing.** it exponentially grew my negotiating skills and my understanding of entrepreneurial thinking. I really thrived under Neville's guidance, and he repaid my efforts by giving me added responsibility. I did five international buying trips in 1989 at the age of 21, flying off to Chicago, Istanbul, Milan, Berlin and Paris. Colorvision was still too small to buy directly from suppliers in Asia, so we used agents and just paid a small commission. So while I didn't get direct exposure to suppliers there, I had extensive links to agents in Hong Kong and the rest of the region.

My knack for numbers also served me well in my work. Growing up in Croxteth, I used to do number tricks for the kids on the street, reciting doubles (1, 2, 4, 8...) all the way up to some ridiculous number like 8 million. At Colorvision I was able to calculate 30 per cent gross margin on prices while knocking out 17.5 per cent VAT in my head. So talking with suppliers, I could pull up figures that left them scratching their heads as to where I'd gotten them. Somewhat less useful, I could also remember the phone number of every store, and recite it faster than someone could look it up or hit speed dial.

I think back to that time and the fact that Neville put tens of millions of pounds of purchasing power in the hands of a 20-year-old, and in many ways it's mind-blowing! Neville told me that he believed in my ability to succeed, and as long as I believed that what I was doing was for the good of the company, I didn't have to ask permission. Talk about trust!

As a result, I became even more driven. I wanted to show that I could produce deal after deal. Neville told me to scour the country and find him the best deals. When he said that to other people, they didn't ignore it, but they just made a couple of trips and few phone calls. But when he told me to scour the country, I spent weeks driving around and talking to potential vendors. And when I came back I told him I'd scoured the country, and I'd found new suppliers 'here, here, here and here'.

As you might expect, some of the people I dealt with were taken aback by my age and position. It would come in various forms, including questions like 'Where's your boss?' or 'Who's the ultimate decision maker?' Sometimes it would be a straightforward question about how old I was. And each time, I would launch into a five-minute monologue with the supplier, asking them if they had a problem with young people in positions of authority. Because Neville had placed his trust in me so early, and because of the negotiation training and skills that he'd passed on, I realised that in every meeting I needed to set the tone and not be disempowered by what I can only call 'ageism'. Generally I would get my message across and negotiations would resume without the issue of my age arising again.

Neville had also started taking me to the electronics tradeshows in London. So we moved around the Cumberland, the Portman, the Dorchester—all the swanky London hotels. The managing directors of brands such as Toshiba and Mitsubishi would pull Neville to one side and ask who I was, and if I wasn't a bit young. Neville would have a bit of fun with that and tell them not to say that to me directly, or they'd regret it.

Although things were going well at Colorvision, I struggled with my relatively low salary. Part of the problem was that I'd started to go on holidays more often with my mates. Eventually, I found that I needed to find a second job to keep myself in the black. As it turned out, this would prove to be a decision that had a major impact on my personal life.

OF BARS TO BABIES

To top up my income a bit, I took a job as a bartender at The Mons, a complex of three bars in Bootle, near the once famous Liverpool docks. I started out in the real 'spit and sawdust' bar, where the customers were mostly old men who wanted their pint of Guinness just so. I was able to get a good relationship going with the old guys and did quite well, which earned me a move to the lounge after just a couple of weeks.

I was happy with the move, but what I really wanted was to get into the fun pub called Breezes, which was where all the action was—loud music, girls with tambourines and lots of dancing—and where a guy my age belonged. Another couple of weeks in the lounge and I convinced the lady who was the boss to let me work in Breezes.

It was during my first week at Breezes that my two work worlds came together for a memorable, but slightly awkward moment. I had just been sent to the island bar for the first time, and was bartending together with eight girls. As a bit of an initiation test, they all ganged up on me at one point and pulled my trousers down, leaving me standing there in my underwear. Now the sensible thing to do would probably have been to pull up my pants and get back to work, but I decided I'd have a bit of fun instead. What did I do? I asked for a tambourine, jumped up on the bar, and started dancing. As you will see, that experience would prove prophetic of how I approached my role as CEO.

As you might imagine, this got a good laugh. But it was right then that my assistant buying clerk and the receptionist from Colorvision walked into the bar. Thankfully I got down off the bar fairly quickly and if anything the incident probably improved my rapport with the two girls from work, though I did ask them not to mention it around the office!

Who says I can't dress up as a Geisha?

Baptism by Fire: Retail Beginnings   47

So I was working at Colorvision during the day and wrapping up around 6 or 6.30, then getting over to the bar at 7 to start work there until 11.30 at night. This wasn't leaving me any time for dinner, and I started stopping off at the Chinese take-away around the corner from the bar on the way home. And that's where I met Janice, who was to become my wife.

Janice was in town from Hong Kong to visit her mother, the take-away owner, for her 50th birthday celebration. We struck up a conversation, and soon I was there pretty much every night chatting her up. I would even go by on weekends, despite the fact that it was quite a bit out of the way from my home. I quickly realised that there were certain items on the menu that would take 20 minutes to be prepared, so I started ordering those to give me a bit more time to hang out in the shop.

Eventually I plucked up the courage to ask her out. To be honest, it wasn't really a date so much as shopping trip; she needed to buy a car and I offered to help her out, since I knew a bit about cars and a thing or two about negotiating from being a buyer at Colorvision. And when she turned up at the car dealership, she arrived with a full entourage—mother, sister, and cousins. Not quite what I had in mind, but it was a start!

On our second date, we managed to get the number of hangers-on down to just one or two, and eventually got a chance to be alone together. That was in late 1987, and things moved rather quickly from there, in part because I knew she was planning to go back to Hong Kong in a few months. When she did go back, I had a feeling that she would return and that the relationship would continue since she had bought a car and, better yet, left me the keys.

Janice did indeed return in early 1988, and we carried on where we'd left off with our whirlwind romance. Then in June we got registered, although we didn't tell anyone except my mate and best man, Aaron, and Janice's sister, Cheryl, who we needed to have along as witnesses. We decided we wanted to keep a more formal church wedding for later, which we did in October 1989.

Once everything was out in the open, we bought a house in Cowley Road (for what now seems like a cheap price of £18,000), right near the Everton football ground. Needless to say I was not amused to have Everton fans streaming past my front door every weekend, particularly as I was staunchly devoted to Liverpool, but beyond that we were quite happy there. By this time my salary at Colorvision had started to rise, so I was able to stop my job at the bar and keep slightly more normal hours. However, our financial situation took a bit of hit about two years later, shortly after we had moved into a new house.

Mike Conboy, the property director at Colorvision, had given me the advice that it was good to get onto the property ladder as early as possible, and to take the maximum mortgage possible. I followed this advice when in 1991 we bought a larger house in a new estate in Cheshire. We had been able to sell the house we bought for £18,000 in Cowley Road for £27,000—a tidy profit in less than two years! The house in Cheshire was a big step up in terms of financial commitment at £74,000. This was fine until interest rates started to skyrocket in the UK, heading well into double figures. For a while more than half my salary was going towards the mortgage!

I can tell you that there is no better motivator than desperation, and that is exactly what I felt when I went in to ask for a pay raise from Neville. As I was trying to justify to him that I should be earning more, I kept thinking: I have to get this. I can't lose this negotiation or I'm in serious trouble. Thankfully, he agreed with me and my salary went up enough to put us back on a comfortable footing.

SHIFTING PERSONAL AND PROFESSIONAL CULTURES

In 1990, at the age of 21, things were clearly going well. I had just married Janice, we had a new home and I was on a roll at work, having been promoted to group buying head. Then in 1991, things began to change at Colorvision. Neville appointed a managing director named Alan Tinger, an ex-corporate affairs director. Alan was brought in to professionalise the company, which had been growing rapidly over the previous few years, but had not always kept up in terms of implementing industry best practices and processes.

> **I can't lose this negotiation.**

Alan taught us about structuring memos and reports, creating organisational charts, and all sorts of other corporate stuff. There was a problem, though—Alan didn't have great people skills. While his intentions were good, and some of the changes he was implementing were needed, he wasn't able to communicate this to the staff. He rubbed a lot of people the wrong way and he also started to recruit some seriously high flyers, which obviously didn't go over too well with the existing team. It wasn't so much the fact that he was looking outside the company for new talent, but that the people he brought in often just weren't very good and, more importantly, they didn't fit into our culture.

He brought in people from some of the big retailers like Dixons, and they seemed more concerned about the car they drove than growing the business. Neville had always drilled into us

> **You're letting him take the lead on company stuff but you're a better leader. Don't let him take away what's special about the company.**

that the company came first. But these guys came in and the first thing they would ask was: What car can I get? Can I change it or upgrade it? I remember one new advertising director sitting down in my office and asking: So what can we get? I was a bit confused, so he clarified, "You know, what can we expense, what is chargeable, what are the benefits, and what kind of freebies can we get on the side?" I was appalled. And I told Neville this.

On one particular occasion—and I'm not sure where I got the courage to say this to him, as I was only 22—I said to Neville, "You built this company. You're a better leader than Alan. But because you lack an advanced degree, and because he's a polished professional, you're letting him take the lead on stuff that you shouldn't. He's taking away what's special about the company, and while we may need to go down a certain route, don't let him take away what's special." On this occasion, as with other times I brought this up, Neville seemed surprised. He would have a word with Alan and tell him to tone things down a bit. But I got the sense that he had yet to see the divisiveness that was running through the company ranks.

What made Colorvision special was the camaraderie created by late-night huddles around the sales figures, chatting about what had happened during the day, and speaking to branch managers on the phone. The group felt very personal, and at the same time we shared a really competitive spirit. We were very used to being David taking on Goliath, with Colorvision taking on much larger players like Dixons. And even though we had grown rapidly from 12 stores to 70 and then to 80 and 90, we were still in many suppliers' eyes a large independent rather than a national chain store. We still felt like family.

This was not to say that I didn't think we needed to change. I knew there was a need for structure and corporate discipline, but at the same time the depersonalisation and ousting of people who had done well for the company was difficult to watch.

I became quite vocal about the situation, and particularly about existing employees losing out on the chance for promotion to imported talent, as I knew that I was on solid ground with Neville due to my performance. I was pretty straightforward with Alan about wanting to become a director. I pushed hard for him to tell me what it would take to get there, and in the end he set some criteria. I then proceeded to achieve those goals, and in 1992 Alan promoted me to buying director. I felt he did so grudgingly, and because the metrics had been achieved he couldn't say no.

I got where I wanted, but I still wasn't happy. The politics at work were starting to come to the fore, and I didn't like how that was playing out.

My instincts proved right. In the end, most of the people brought in were fired after Neville realised that their contributions were superficial. At one point, one of our marketing directors came into my office and said he'd just been let go. When I asked him why, he told me that the board suggested that he should come and ask me. Then we just sat down and had the first real conversation that we'd ever had.

I suggested to him that he hadn't taken the time to learn the culture of the company, or participate with colleagues in developing advertising campaign strategies. The team carried on with their work as if he hadn't joined. This gave him quite a shock, but he gave what felt like a sincere thank you when he went out the door.

> **LESSON**
>
> **Recognise that any employee's objective has to be to add value to the business.** Therefore, your attitude to company expenses defines your attitude towards the company. I have found that executives who approach their job with the mindset of getting something out of the company—whether it be perks, benefits or expense reimbursement—often offer the worst job performance. They spend far too much energy worrying about what the company owes them, when what they could be focusing on is how they can perform better to help the company succeed.

THE ASIA 'BUG'

The result of all this upheaval was that I realised that I needed to be in a position where I could project greater influence on the culture of an organisation. I also realised that the only way I would be fully valued would be if I were brought into an organisation as their imported talent. So the seeds of change had been planted in my mind and I started to consider what my next move would be.

Early in 1991, Janice and I decided we wanted to have a baby. But before we did that, we thought it would be good to go for a holiday together, so we planned a trip to Asia. We visited Thailand, Hong Kong and Beijing. It was a fantastic trip and I met with some suppliers and agents in Hong Kong—not for business, but just to say hello and have a chat. It was at this point that I started to get the Asia bug. I saw that there was clearly a lot going on in Asia, and that it could be a very interesting and exciting place to live and work.

After having our son Daniel in February 1992, I got serious about finding my next job. I was not initially looking for a position in Asia, but rather for companies in the UK with international links. I think the possibility of a wholesale move to Asia had not really occurred to me yet. I had a no-compete clause at Colorvision, which I was naïve to enough to think could actually be enforced, but a bigger reason for thinking about overseas options was that I couldn't imagine ending up in a competitive situation against my mentor Neville. It was going to be hard enough leaving the company, I certainly didn't want to end up competing against it!

Over the next few months I had discussions with a number of companies and nearly took jobs with one or two of them, but ultimately didn't feel they were quite right. As I continued exploring the job market, I was also increasingly leaning towards finding an Asia-based job. I had come to the realisation that this made a lot of sense. I had a Chinese wife, I loved Asia, and I was dealing with a lot of suppliers that were brokering and sourcing products in Asian markets. So Asia just seemed to be the logical choice and I initially set my sights on Hong Kong. I was really impressed with the city when we were there and it seemed to be the place for electronics buying. I also felt that it was where I was most likely to land a job given my skill sets and background.

I went to the annual trade shows in London again and came to learn through some of my contacts that Ged Dempsey, who had just joined Courts Plc, a UK retailer, as head of central buying, was building regional buying teams. To start with, I had no idea what Courts was—it had all its stores in southern England and only took out ads in southern papers, so there wasn't any exposure to them in Liverpool. But I decided to contact Ged, as I had heard of him, and it turned out that he had heard of me as well. We agreed that I would go down to London to meet him.

So I went in to see Ged, and he turned out to be this jovial Irishman. It wasn't really an interview so much as a chat. We swapped industry stories, a bit of gossip, and generally just chewed the fat. Later that night he called me and said he wanted me to meet the chairman and the CEO the following week. This turned out to be a kind of odd, very casual interview situation. I went in very confident because the thought of separating from Neville absolutely terrified me, so I was in a situation where I didn't really care if I got the job or not. In the back of my head, I was probably thinking that if I didn't get the job, I would be avoiding the difficult situation of telling Neville I was leaving.

This lack of concern about whether I would impress them or not must have unleashed something inside me, because I gave it to them double-barrels—telling them what they should be doing and what they were doing wrong. Despite my over-confidence and what I guess was a slight lack of decorum, I hit it off with Courts' chairman, Paul Cohen. A few days later I got a call from his brother Bruce, the CEO, and he offered me the job of electrical buying director for Singapore. Simple as that.

I decided to talk to Alan about my departure first. I felt that talking to Neville would be too emotional, and that he would try to convince me to stay. I was pretty sure Alan would accept my resignation and that he could then break the news to Neville. I spoke to Alan while Neville was away on a trip, and I asked him to tell Neville that my mind was made up and that I didn't want him to try and convince me to stay.

Then Neville came back and we didn't speak for a few days. And when we did speak, it was not mentioned. And then a few days later he said, "You know Alan's told me about the conversation you've had. I've been advised not to try to persuade you to stay." I then told him that it was a great opportunity and that my leaving wasn't up for negotiation, to which he replied, "Ok, I'm proud of you." To say I didn't have a lump in my throat at that point would be a lie.

> **One of the key lessons I took from Neville was to do what I wanted to do as long as I was doing it for the right reasons and the good of the business.**

And that was about it until about a week before I was due to leave. Then one day Neville stopped me in the car park and he said, "Ok, this is ridiculous, you need to stay. I will give you a blank cheque and you can write your amount on it." Tempting as this may have sounded, I explained to him that it wasn't about money; that I'd made a commitment and I was excited about it. I then said that I had fond memories of my time at Colorvision and that it was going to be a really emotional departure, so I preferred that he didn't make it more difficult. And that settled it.

We had a leaving party with my staff, and after all was said and done, Neville walked off. I don't know for sure, but there was an employee, Pauline, in the office who said he was in tears in the corridor. As for me, I sobbed all the way home. I had just closed an important chapter of my life, but I was on the verge of a new, exciting journey.

CHAPTER 3
The Incongruities of a Family-Run Global Business

Joining a new company always involves being thrust into a new organisational culture. But when I joined Courts, I was unprepared for simultaneous feelings of familiarity and alienation. While Courts was keen to venture into the relatively new retail territory of electronics, its family-run management retained a very old-school feel and old-school attitudes. Adding me to the mix—a self-starter from the streets of Liverpool—only added to the incongruities. But it is cultural boundaries like these that I have become adept at bridging: a quality that I believe is essential to any successful manager or company. As you will learn below, stepping into unknown territory has more than once transformed Courts for the better.

When I went for my interview with the Cohens at Courts in 1993, I was struck by the thick pile carpets, a dining room staffed with tea ladies, and offices in an old Tudor manor house called 'The Grange' that dated back to 1554! Bruce Cohen, the CEO, was called 'Mr Bruce' and Paul Cohen, Bruce's cousin and Courts' chairman, was 'Mr Paul'. Many of the staff had been with Courts for decades.

This is not to say that I have something against long-serving staff—we've got plenty of those at Courts in Singapore! The eccentricities of the Courts management in part emanated from the company's history. At Courts in the UK, it was more a case of time having stood still. It quickly became apparent to me that the workplace was not particularly progressive. People had come in with a certain skills set but did little to keep up to date with the evolution of the markets outside The Grange's sturdy walls. Similarly, it was clear that there hadn't been much investment in modernising the office. There were few if any computers and most processes were still done manually.

Paul came across to me as the patriarch of the organisation. He seemed comfortable overseeing the organisation and those who served it. Bruce Cohen was a charming man, but in my opinion was not as comfortable with confrontation. Instead of firing underperforming employees, he would move them to smaller markets. Once he promised two managers the same job. He made good on his promise, but it wasn't a good business decision. This was just one example of how Bruce's effort to keep employees happy turned out to be bad for Courts' operations.

Meanwhile, the deputy CEO, Howard Cohen (Bruce Cohen's brother), was perhaps the more eccentric member of the family. He was more interested in knowing about how our stores controlled indoor temperatures or what colour the buildings were painted for energy preservation purposes. I remember seeing him give lessons to people on the shop floor about electricity conduction by getting staff to hold hands to get a light bulb to turn on. Not exactly the duties of deputy CEO, but endearing nonetheless.

The eccentricities of the Courts' management are understandable when you consider the company's history. Courts originated in Canterbury, England, in 1850, as a small family-owned shop selling kettles and pots. The owner, Albert Court, spent several decades with his sons William and Charles expanding store merchandise. They introduced ironmongery, oil, paints, bicycles, hardware, furniture and furnishings. I would throw in the saying here about how they sold 'everything but the kitchen sink', but they probably sold those too! Following a practice that was common at the time, they opened a number of workshops to supply the store with its own line of bedding, cabinetry, carpeting and curtains, and paint. At one point Courts even bought a windmill to grind pigments for its paints!

By 1900, the business—workshops and oil distribution services included—employed some 120 staff. Pictures of the Burgate Street store from around 1904 show Court Bros., as the company was then known, to have a wide, attractive storefront displaying everything from blinds, upholstery and sewing machines to chinaware, glass and pottery. By all accounts Courts' reputation grew together with the size of its store, and it became renowned for its quality, good value and helpful service.

Burgate Street, 1905

The business continued to flourish throughout the 1920s, when the next generation of Courts, William's sons Henry and Percy, joined the management team. Following the death of his brother Charles in 1931, William split

Courts into two separate businesses: Court Bros. (Builders Merchants) Limited, headed by Henry, and Court Bros. (Furnishers) Limited, led by Percy. When William died a year later the Builders Merchants business took a turn for the worse, and Henry sold it off to another firm and moved his family to North Devon to settle into a quiet life running a small general store there.

Percy, on the other hand, proved to have a flair for retailing and quickly expanded the shop's showrooms. But Courts took some hits during economic struggles of the 1930s and later, by the second World War. By 1945, Court Bros. had been whittled down to a staff of just eight and Percy decided to sell the business to three brothers, Henry, Alfred and Edwin Cohen. This was a pivotal turning point.

FROM LONDON TO JAMAICA: A NEW ERA IN FURNITURE RETAIL

Within three years, the Cohens had expanded Courts from its original shop in Canterbury to six High Street stores. They proceeded to open two to three new stores every year and by 1959 counted 34 retail stores concentrated in the south and south east of England. In the process of building its business, the company had established itself as a leading hire purchase company and had listed on the London Stock Exchange in 1959.

In the late 1950s and the 1960s, the second generation of Cohens—those whom I would get to know when I joined Courts—was starting to enter the business. Paul Cohen was the first of this group, joining in 1956. He was followed by Bruce Cohen in 1964, and these two ended up respectively becoming the chairman and CEO of Courts in the 1980s. Howard Cohen later also joined as deputy CEO.

Things were clearly going well for the business. However, the Cohen brothers were concerned about the risks associated with having all their stores in England, so they began to consider overseas expansion. They had no specific countries in mind, but knew they were looking for English-speaking locations where they could easily send their staff to train local employees. All they needed was an opportunity.

A chance meeting in 1958 between Edwin Cohen and a retired English soldier named George Webb delivered just what they were looking for. Webb met Cohen to discuss the purchase of furniture and house wares for a hotel he was opening in Jamaica. Webb told Edwin that Jamaica was lacking in quality furniture stores, and he suggested that

Courts should open a store there—probably as far-fetched an idea as could have been suggested to a staid English company at the time! But the Courts' management at the time took the 'why not?' attitude approach to the idea, and Edwin and his wife combined a holiday and exploratory business trip to the island to test the Caribbean waters. Webb introduced Edwin to several influential people and helped him secure an option for a parcel of suitable land. A number of trans-Atlantic phone calls later, and the Cohen brothers decided to proceed with investing £57,000 in the building of a 26,000 square foot retail and warehouse facility on the outskirts of Kingston, Jamaica.

When I first joined Courts, two of my colleagues had been amongst the UK staff sent to Kingston to help with the store set-up and management. They were probably no more than 19 or 20 years old at that time, and they had some fond memories of the posting, recalling that it was an exciting time.

Courts had initially intended to export only its brand and its expertise to Jamaica, and depend on local furniture manufacturers and, with the exception of a couple senior managers, hire local residents to staff the stores. But when they started developing the business in Jamaica, it quickly became clear that Courts would have to rely initially on imports from the UK. The local industry was too immature to support Courts' operations. Although this was considered something of a setback, it inadvertently worked to Courts' advantage, as it was able to introduce furniture of a level of quality and style that Jamaica had not seen.

Courts' first Jamaican store, the Cross Roads branch, opened in May 1959 and thereafter quickly exceeded targets for sales and profitability. In addition to offering unique, high-quality products, Courts also offered hire purchase, just as its stores in the UK did. Through this service, customers were able to buy 'the home of their dreams' on affordable terms. And Courts' terms were significantly better than what was available from other stores on the island—20 per cent deposit, 18 months to pay the balance and free delivery, versus 33 per cent, 12 months and no delivery. You can guess which one the customers preferred!

Courts became something of a pioneer in the industry in Jamaica, in terms of both products and financing. At that time, many Jamaicans were buying their first large home appliances, such as refrigerators and washing machines, but they wanted credit to finance the purchases. According to Courts' company lore, customers began asking if they could put a fridge or similarly priced item—on their account. The local branch manager would go and buy a fridge from another shop at a bit of a discount and sell it to the customer on credit. At some point someone must have realised that there was a business there and started to bring electricals into the stores. In this roundabout way, Courts stumbled into electrical retailing in the 1980s—just as the business was about to take off.

Meanwhile, in furniture, Courts' policy of buying locally gradually became a reality, Courts was able to offer quality products at even lower prices. In 1959, its stock had been 80 per cent imported products and 20 per cent local, but by 1965 it had reversed these shares, with the vast majority of its wares produced locally.

The initial and quite immediate success of the Cross Roads store led to the opening of a second Jamaican Courts branch in Mandeville in 1960, which proved to be equally successful. These two stores whet the appetite of the Cohens, and they began to think more seriously about further international expansion. In 1965 they made their next overseas foray by opening a store in Bridgetown, Barbados.

As an indication of the novelty of Courts' presence in Barbados, the 16,000 square foot store and warehouse was opened by the Prime Minister, Mr Errol Barrow, and met with enthusiastic approval from the general public. Landing in Barbados two days before the opening, Edmund Cohen drove past the site of the new store on his way from the airport to the hotel and was amazed to see crowds four-deep trying to get a glimpse of the wares displayed in the shop windows.

While the store in Bridgetown was a success, the relatively small market in Barbados appeared to limit the potential for growth of the business. Rather than settle for a good share of the island's smallish furniture and furnishing business, the directors at Courts decided to expand the store's product range. For the first time in Courts' modern era, they introduced domestic appliances, sewing machines and bicycles—something of a return to the product diversity of the original Courts on Burgate Street in the late 1800s! Given that electronics were taking off across most developed economies, it was no surprise that Courts' expanded product range found an eager market. Courts applied the same product strategy to the majority of Courts' overseas stores from that point forward.

The success in Jamaica led Courts to list its subsidiary's shares on the local stock market in 1969, and this proved a significant move, as it tied Courts even more closely to the Jamaican market and signalled a clear commitment to growing operations not just there, but also in the region.

Courts would eventually have more than 30 stores in Jamaica, and expansion throughout the 1970s, 80s and 90s resulted in some 120 stores in the Caribbean accounting for 27 per cent of the company's total sales at the turn of the century.

ISLAND HOPPING

At the same time that expansion in the Caribbean was taking place, Asia-Pacific was also seeing its fair share of new Courts stores. From its home base in London, the Cohen brothers directed the opening of stores in Fiji and Australia in 1970 and Singapore in 1974, before moving into Papua New Guinea, Malaysia, Indonesia, and Hong Kong in subsequent decades. Asia-Pacific became the third pillar of the Courts global empire, as it were.

It's worth noting here that the Cohens had by no means forsaken their home market in the UK during this period of international expansion (something they may well have regretted later on!). By 1980, there were 98 Courts stores spanning southern England and Wales.

Not all of the overseas ventures during this time were huge successes. In general, Courts did well going into developing markets where the credit financing model was popular and provided a strong profit source. More developed markets that were based on cash business did less well (with the one exception being Singapore). For example, Australia was in and out of profit for 16 years and never made a lot of money, and Hong Kong stores proved unsuccessful and were eventually shut down.

THE TENSIONS IN BEING A HOMEBODY ABROAD

Interestingly, overseas expansion exposed a weakness in the group's management policies: many Directors who managed their overseas businesses were uncomfortable mixing into the fabric of local economies. In fact, most of the Board managed their overseas operations remotely from the UK. For example, Australia was one of the few markets in the Courts empire where the Cohens posted a family member to run the business. This has puzzled me over the years. In my mind, if you're running what is essentially a family business, and you've got 20 or so markets and five key family members in senior management, you'd position those members across the biggest markets. The Cohens, however, were pretty much all based in the UK, and would go on yearly visits to different markets that were labelled as 'consultant director visits'.

This is not to say that Courts' leaders were not good at expansion—you don't build a global empire without knowing a thing or two about going into new markets. They were very astute at selecting markets for entry and would put a lot of work into understanding the markets before going in. But once they were there, they often didn't put in place the kind of senior management infrastructure you might expect. I think this resulted in losing out on learning opportunities in these new markets that could have been applied to the UK business further down the road that could have kept it out of the troubles it would later face.

Singapore was one of the successful markets for Courts. Its entry here came in 1974, when it opened a store on Orchard Road, just opposite the Istana, the President's official residence. A road-widening project forced Courts out of that store four years later, and saw it relocate to Bukit Timah Road, where the new store opened in March 1979. At the time, Courts Singapore was led by Christopher Wade, who had been sent here in 1974 to prepare for the opening, and stayed on as managing director until 1990.

In 1990, Albert Elphick, who served as managing director until 1996, replaced Wade. Albert was in charge when I joined the company in 1993 and was posted to Singapore.

COURTS OVERSEAS EXPANSION

1958 – Jamaica
1965 – Barbados
1970 – Fiji and Australia
1972 – Hong Kong
1974 – Singapore
1980 – Guernsey and Jersey
1981 – St Lucia
1983 – Papua New Guinea
1985 – Mauritius, Antigua and Barbuda
1987 – Malaysia and Grenada
1991 – Trinidad and Tobago
1992 – Dominica
1995 – Indonesia
1996 – Belize and Ireland
1997 – St Kitts
1998 – St Vincent, The Grenadines
1999 – Bequia, The Grenadines
2001 – Madagascar
2003 – Thailand

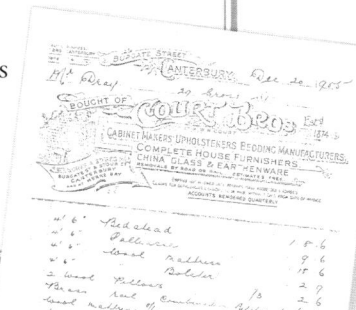

The early days

FIRST DAYS AT COURTS

I started at Courts' London office on the Monday following my last day at Colorvision. It was a bit of a surreal experience that first day, as there was quite literally no induction programme, no structure, and nobody to report to. I got an office and a desk and a couple of loose appointments, but that was it.

At that time, Courts was hiring staff to help professionalise its electrical retail business. It quickly became apparent that while we were doing quite well in electricals, the management around the category was surprisingly disorganised. It lacked formal processes, and some operations seemed to be running themselves. In Singapore, for example, the manager running electricals (in addition to furniture) was adept commercially, but didn't seem to understand some of the key processes in electricals, such as formal ranging and vendor management.

To be fair, the electrical side of the business was fairly new for Courts.

I spent my first few weeks at Courts not in Singapore, but at the Cohen family villa in Barbados, where I'd been sent to help with an electrical refit in the main store there—a job that had little to do with my role as electricals buyer for the Singapore market. The two-storey villa employed a full staff that included a chef and a gardener. It was also equipped with a golf course and a library with books that looked about a century old. And that impression foreshadowed the tensions between old and new that would afflict Courts' business in coming years.

We got to Barbados on Sunday to start the project on Monday. Another employee who was helping with the refit was sunbathing by the pool, and I foolishly decided to do the same. As it turns out, the Irish and excessive sunshine don't really mix, and my ankle blew up like a golf ball. So I ended up helping with the refit while sitting across two chairs with my leg up, just screwing in fixtures that they would bring me. I got a bit of a ribbing about that a week later when we were back in the UK. Not exactly a glorious start!

ALWAYS SOMETHING UNNERVING ABOUT MEETING THE BOSS, ESPECIALLY WHEN ONE'S BOSS IS UNNERVING

Back in London, Bruce came by and told me that Albert Elphick, the Singapore managing director, was in town, and that he'd like me to join them for dinner. Like the Cohens, Albert had a long history with Courts. His father had been with Courts in Australia, and his grandfather had been working at Court Bros. when the Cohens bought it in 1947. In fact, his family's involvement in the company actually predated the Cohens. Albert's son followed him into the business, and I recently learned that *his* son has joined Courts in Papua New Guinea. That's five generations of the family in the Courts business!

My first words from the boss were: "We were 105 per cent up last week—beat that!"

Albert had a long history with Courts, and when I mentioned to a few people at the office that I was going to meet my new boss that evening, I felt disturbed when I noticed some hesitation in their reaction. I soon found out why: Albert was extremely competitive.

My first meeting with Albert began with no 'hello', no formal introduction. Instead, as I walked into Bruce's house to meet him Albert pointed to me and said, "We were 105 per cent up last week—beat that!" Not quite the greeting I was expecting. I didn't get any comfort during our meeting, either, as Albert torched every single of my admittedly naïve questions.

Following our meeting, Albert gave me a lift back to the hotel. Along the way, he asked me what kind of car I was driving, and I replied that I had a Ford Granada

Scorpio, which was Ford's top model at the time. He replied to the effect that I wouldn't have anything like that in Singapore. Rather, he said something to the effect that I'd have a run-of-the-mill Hyundai Pony, and that I'd like it. I didn't particularly care what kind of car I was driving, but Albert made several comments like this on the way back to the hotel that seemed to be said in a tone meant to put me in my place.

I realised that if this was just the beginning, then it was going to be a bit of a problem. When we got to the hotel, I asked him to join me for a drink. I acknowledged that he hadn't hired me, so maybe he felt I had been thrust on him, or perhaps he didn't agree with my being hired. But I told him very clearly that he was my boss, and I would work for him. "Whatever I achieve, I'm trying to achieve it to impress you. And if there are any ground rules or concerns or things I have to abide by, then I'm happy to know about it and abide by it." He seemed to relax a bit after that and we finished the evening with a few more drinks. This was by no means the end of issues between us, but it did set the tone for the next three years.

CONNECTING THE NOT-SO-DISSIMILAR LIVERPOOL AND SINGAPORE CULTURES

After this abrupt introduction to my new boss, our family prepared to head to Singapore. Our son Daniel, who had been born in February 1992, made us a party of three.

Looking back at what Singapore was like at the time I arrived, I'm struck by how different it is today, although I realise this is to be expected from one of Asia's true Tiger economies. That said, it was a lot more modern than I expected it to be. For those of you who know Singapore, Ngee Ann City—a major shopping centre—was just being built, and Boat Quay, the restaurant and night club hub, had only just opened. There was an international flavour creeping into Singapore, but it wasn't as full on as you see today. In fact, my first few days probably exposed me to the older, colonial side of Singapore more than anything else. Albert and his partner took me to the Tanglin Club—a bastion of Singapore's colonial days if ever there was one—for dinner on my first night in town.

What I think is more interesting is some of the ways of doing business at that time. For example, suppliers were still having tradeshows with free-flow beer, bottoms-up toasts, and handing the order forms to unseasoned buyers to fill in over drinks. Business relations seemed to centre around hard drinking—and every supplier, agent and contractor wanted to take me out for karaoke and sit me down next to a hostess. At some point I got so fed up with it that I put my foot down and decided I was done with karaoke. I remember telling one of our suppliers that I wasn't interested in sitting around a karaoke lounge with a bunch of pretty girls and feeling awkward, and that I was taking him out for a good pint of Guinness at the Irish pub, Muddy Murphy's. I think he appreciated the introduction to Irish beer, and I felt it did much more for our relationship to be able to sit down and have a meaningful conversation rather than fight to be heard over loud, tinny music.

There were many other practices that I considered to be outdated, and I have to admit that I probably came in and shook things up a little. I remember taking all of my branch managers and making them sit up at the front at trade events. That was something Neville taught me. He said that we were a market leader, so we needed to be up front and visible. This added to the drama at a particular event hosted by a major Japanese brand, when I got everyone from Courts to walk out after ten minutes because we were told that if we wanted to participate in a particular promotion, we had to purchase a specific product package from them. I thought, 'Why do I need to buy a package just to participate in your promotion? We're a big retailer.' And so we walked out. This resulted in some shock and disbelief on the supplier's side. I guess they weren't used to such opposition from their clients—but before we even got out the door they came after us saying that they were willing to compromise.

In retrospect, I did plenty of somewhat rash things in my early years in Singapore. Sometimes I look back now and think, *bloody hell, I don't think I'd do that now*—my 'why not?' nature, notwithstanding. Much of my behaviour exacerbated my already tense relationship with Albert. At the same time, though, some of my actions—including building a strong, loyal team—created positive change at Courts.

CHAPTER 4

Singapore Fling

Introducing change can be a sensitive issue, regardless of how good your intentions or how obvious it is that change is needed. An effective change manager needs to know when to apply a light touch, and when to get out the sledgehammer.

Before I arrived in Singapore, my only impression of Courts' Singapore operations came from a large photograph of its Bukit Timah store showing three stories of floor space covering 20,000 square feet each. Colorvision stores were typically about 1,000 square feet. This one store was much larger than anything I had been responsible for at Colorvision, and I was a bit apprehensive about whether I could manage the buying for such a large operation.

These fears were quickly allayed when I arrived at the Bukit Timah store on the Monday that I began work in Singapore. My eyes took in an array of inventory placed haphazardly across the floor and back offices with stacks of unsorted paperwork. Things like allocating a sale to a product and checking special incentives for the shop floor were still being done manually!

Inventory haphazardly splayed across the floor and stacks of unsorted paperwork ... This was to be the first of a number of shocks.

I also discovered that the team of eight buyers that I would be supervising consisted not of buyers, exactly, but of seven delivery staff and one assistant buyer, a local employee named Sandy. The trouble was, Sandy was the only Chinese person in the office and kept getting roped into talking to Chinese customers about deliveries, which left her with little time to help me liaise with suppliers and coordinate purchases in her assistant buyer role. I felt like I had half a staff member. This was to be the first of a number of shocks as I found out more about how Courts Singapore operated.

I remember writing a letter home to friends saying that I thought this job was going to be easy, despite the fact that I'd been a little bit daunted going in. But when I observed

Courts' operations, I thought to myself: *This is great! It's a successful business with plenty of room for improvement. And there's no better position to be in than to join a successful business that is easily improved.*

TRANSFORMING SOFAS TO SOUND SYSTEMS

When I joined Courts, its electricals business was already bigger than the furniture business in its overseas markets. The problem was that electricals weren't making any money, at least not on the actual product sales. In Singapore, electricals accounted for about two-thirds of annual revenues but only 40 per cent of gross profits, while furniture made up one-third of annual revenues and 60 per cent of gross profits. Courts' management recognised the problem and assigned Ged Dempsey, my first contact at Courts, to sort out the electricals business and put it in the black.

To do this, he and his team in London developed strategies for each market and then parachuted the group of us that he'd recently hired into the individual markets to start turning things around. One of the key problems with Courts' existing electricals business was that the people running it didn't have electricals backgrounds. Instead, as

Courts businesses around the world had gradually moved into electricals, it was people from the existing furniture business—in some cases, the country's managing director—who had taken up the job of buying. However, since they didn't have experience in electricals, they often didn't know what to order, what to negotiate, etc.

My primary responsibility was to transform Singapore's electricals business. And it turned out to be a terrific challenge.

SHAKING UP THE SHOP FLOOR

Improving store sales across Singapore, for example, turned out to be more difficult than I expected. Our Bukit Timah store—the largest in Singapore, located in the middle of the island—was not delivering to its potential. Product displays were done by brand, and every inch of the shop floor was covered by a stand: a Sony stand, a Panasonic stand, a Kenwood stand, etc. To allow room for a new supplier, we would first have to get rid of an existing stand. And the process for that, I was informed, could take up to six weeks! I had thought the brand management approach had gone the way of the dinosaur, but apparently that extinction hadn't reached our stores.

Since products were not managed by category, the store was basically like a trade fair. A customer wanting to compare TV screen quality, for example, would have to walk all over the store from stand to stand. Clearly, it was time for change.

I went in to see Albert, our managing director, and told him I really wanted to change the shop floor so that the displays were by category rather than by brand. He said no, and he was adamant. I suggested that we could try making minor changes to display management during our upcoming renovation of the Bukit Timah store, but Albert shot this down straight away. There were probably a few reasons for his opposition.

First, brand management was familiar and it was how things were done at Courts Singapore, so to Albert it was probably a question of: if it ain't broke, don't fix it. Second, he was likely concerned about the costs involved. Under brand management, each brand would pay for installing its own stand in our stores, so if we did away with this approach, it would likely mean additional costs to Courts for fitting out the stores. Third, and perhaps most importantly, Albert probably saw my suggestion as a form of external interference originating from the UK or from Ged, and thus his natural reaction was to protect his territory from outside meddling.

> **I was basically shaking things up because the way that a lot of things had been done up to then just didn't make sense to me.**

As disappointing as this was, I wasn't about to give up. I knew category management was a far superior system and thought if I could just get a chance to demonstrate this with some real results, Albert would change his mind.

In the spirit of 'why not?', my next strategy was to ask Albert to let me renovate one of our smallest stores with relatively low turnover, in Paya Lebar. I thought that Albert might object to the associated cost, so I proposed that I would try to get the store renovation fully paid for by our suppliers, including the costs related to advertising the re-launch of the store. I would arrange it so that the changes wouldn't cost the company a cent. This seemed to work for Albert, and he grudgingly said to go ahead.

I was pleased with this small concession and got right to work. To be honest, it wasn't all that small, because while the Paya Lebar store was our smallest, the renovations included opening up the second floor of the shop, which would increase the floor area to 34,000 square feet. Not a bad space for my category management pilot project!

This was in July, and the launch of the renovated Paya Lebar store was coming up in September, so I dove in and got to work. This is not to say that I wasn't busy before getting this project. Those first two months in Singapore I was like a bullet out of a gun, drinking about 10 cans of Red Bull a day and doing 20 things at once. I reviewed every aspect of our electrical buying procedures and wrote to suppliers saying we wanted better trading terms, we wanted more financial support and we wanted advance supplier briefings of new merchandise. I was basically shaking things up because the way that a lot of things had been done up to then just didn't make sense to me. Looking back, it was a bit like mayhem, really. It was all managed with sense and sensitivity, but we just did a lot of stuff and it took a huge amount of energy.

To proceed with the Paya Lebar store renovation, we requested suppliers take the money that they would use to bear the costs of a product stand and pay us a credit note instead. We didn't need the stand, but we did want financial support, including funding for advertising. This was a huge change in direction, and it took quite a bit of convincing to make it all work. In the end, we had to make some compromises that moved away from being 100 per cent category management-based by allowing a few brand-sponsored concept corners. While this allowed a handful of suppliers to shine spotlight on their brands, these concept corners were much smaller in scale than the areas of the store that we used to allocate to them under the previous brand management setup. In addition, we were able to charge these suppliers a sponsorship fee for the exclusive rights to the concept corner—for example, a major Japanese audio brand paid $100,000 to sponsor a sound room featuring their audio equipment.

When everything was said and done, we even had a little bit of a surplus, which I put into the price of the launch specials, cutting many product prices by half. Previous store openings offered free balloons, free popcorn and things like that. I just wanted lower prices. I figured the best way to expose potential customers to new displays was to get them to come in, in droves.

The strategy worked: before the renovation, the Paya Lebar store's record weekly turnover had been about $320,000, but in that launch week we brought in $966,000. But on the first day back in the office after the launch, Albert said nothing—no 'well-done', no 'great job'. He didn't acknowledge our success until the regular Tuesday morning advertising meeting, when he said, simply, that the renovated store's first week results were great, and that the electrical merchandising was exceptional. He said nothing more about it. Nonetheless, he must have been impressed: Courts employed the same category management strategies in all subsequent renovations of Singapore stores.

This episode was representative of my dealings with Albert throughout the time that we worked together. He never backed down in the face of a confrontation, but would be instantly appeased if he felt that you were aligning to his view.

All of this is not to say that Albert wasn't a good manager in many respects. He was a great networker and he was incredibly good at the detail of Singapore. For example, he was very smart on the property side of the business and managed to secure us some great store locations. He was also a good cost controller, although there were definitely times when I didn't agree with his views regarding costs and investing in the business. For example, while Albert did a fine job of achieving top-line growth by expanding the business, I felt that he didn't invest enough in the back-end infrastructure needed to support this front-end expansion.

Ultimately, I think our relationship worked out well for the company, because I don't mind being pushed. Being challenged triggers my 'why not?' attitude, and pushes me to give 120 per cent, much like I did when Neville placed huge amounts of responsibility on my shoulders at Colorvision. I was always intent on delivering to Albert more than he asked for.

One of the core takeaways from my work at Colorvision with Neville—the words that really resonated, and they were among the first words he ever said to me—was to do what I wanted to do as long as I was doing it for the right reasons and the good of the business. Many times during those early years at Courts I would come back to this thought. It became my guiding mantra.

As I explained to my team at Courts, if we wanted to get anything done, we first needed to sell it to Albert. Although this could be frustrating at times—we needed his approval for everything, even to buy the department's first-ever fax machine—we did manage to get things done: my first three years in Singapore were a very successful period for Courts, despite a couple of unexpected hiccups.

LEARNING TO BLOW THE WHISTLE WITHOUT MAKING WAVES

For instance, early on I became friends with our finance director, who seemed to me to be always looking a bit stressed. One day, I figured out why. The stocktaking results showed a stock loss of $600,000 for the past six months—a stunning amount on an electrical stockholding of somewhere between $6 million and $8 million. I then found out that we'd lost an equivalent amount in the six months before that too. Clearly, something was wrong. The group that I was discussing this with suggested that there must be something wrong with the inventory system. But to me it was clear that we were dealing with a case of theft.

I took the issue to Albert, but he wasn't prepared to accept it as a case of theft and not a systems issue. This one was of the strange paradoxes about him—for someone who came across as a relatively hard guy, he didn't want to rock the boat by firing people, even when the company had apparently suffered a stock loss of $1.2 million over the past year. I decided to set this aside for a while, but knew that I would have to return to it sooner or later.

> **There is corruption in this room, I just don't know which one of you is responsible, but I will find out.**

About two months later, I had to go back to England for some meetings at the head office. While I was there, Michael Hacker, the group finance director, pulled me aside and asked what I was doing about the stock loss problem. I explained that there seemed to be a lack of acceptance that we have a problem, and that I didn't feel senior enough to take it on independently. That said, I told him I did want to get to the bottom of it, but if he wanted me to fix it, I needed to be empowered to fix it.

On my first Monday back in the Singapore office, Albert buzzed me to come to his office. He wanted to know what I had been saying to Michael Hacker. I explained that Michael challenged me on the stock loss and I had told him I'd be happy to take it on if he (Albert) wanted me to take it on. After a bit of discussion, he told me to go ahead and fix it.

Of course, I had no proof that it was theft. But I knew that the only way to deal with theft is to change processes, make people personally accountable, and get the potential candidates into a room to discuss it and see what shakes out. I thought it likely that the thief was either the person who orders the product, the person who checks it into stock or the person who stores it—point of order, point of entry, point of storage. One of these three people was a crook, I just didn't know which one. So I called them all in—the warehouse manager, the storekeeper and Sandy, my assistant buyer.

I explained that I knew one of them was contributing to this. It was a bit like a movie, really, and I felt like an inspector gathering everyone in a room to explain the case, "There is corruption in this room, I just don't know which one of you is responsible, but I will find out." I appeared to know a lot more than I actually did, but that was the whole point. Once I was done, I sent them out and decided to wait two hours to see what happened.

Within a couple of hours Christina Quek, the manager of our Paya Lebar store, called me. She thought I should know that she was being asked to take in a number of laser disc players and to book them back in when she hadn't sent them out in the first place. The key question, of course, was who had asked her to do this. And it turned out to be Sandy. I asked Christina to keep quiet about this and waited a week to see what else came out of the woodwork. With a bit of further investigation, it became clear that Sandy had been placing orders and sending stock directly to her brother's shop.

This left me with the unfortunate situation of turning in Sandy for theft, and that left me with no buying team at all. In the midst of this operation, I also fired three or four delivery contractors and their teams who just seemed to be lurking around our stores, and I changed some other members of the warehousing and storekeeping teams. In total, I removed 17 people. The good news was that at the next stock count, the loss was $50,000, which is normal for the volume of merchandise we were handling.

REBUILDING THE BUYING TEAM

I was now in search of people to start rebuilding my team and I started by looking for a buyer and a stock controller. One of our best store managers, Emily Koh at our Kallang store, showed some promise as a buyer. And one of our suppliers, Sharp, had recommended a woman who was particularly good at stock control. This is an example of where a bit of office politics came into play, as I knew that Albert was close with the Sharp general manager, which I thought made it more likely that he would approve the hire.

So I went to Albert with my plan to bring both Emily and Susie into my team. The trouble was that store managers were paid four to five times as much as Sandy had been paid as assistant buyer. Even with paying Susie at the market rate for a stock controller, I was asking Albert to increase my payroll bill by about eightfold. When he said that Emily was too expensive, I countered by saying that $1.2 million in losses was quite a high cost too. After a bit of negotiating and encouraging, Albert finally gave his approval to hire Emily as my buyer and Susie as my stock controller. The start of my first proper buying team!

The pace of sales then picked up, and I persuaded Albert to get a second buyer. Emily was then helping me on the commercial side with deals, a new recruit, Choon Gek, was handling the buying, while Susie was controlling the stock. Those were heady days for me. We were growing really quickly and with every store opening—now with category management in place—we were hitting the ball out of the park. Our sales were setting record after record after record.

While my team was hitting its stride, I was using a lot of what I had picked up from Neville to boost morale and create a strong teamwork ethic. I was taking my team out for beers, karaoke (of the fun group-singing variety, not the karaoke hostess lounge variety I was dragged to by suppliers upon my arrival in Singapore) and other bonding activities. It felt a bit like a sub-culture within Courts Singapore. What I was doing was definitely not part of the corporate culture. At one point Albert told me not to get too close to the staff. By this time I knew better than to challenge him on this, but I carried on teambuilding nonetheless. I also began thinking harder about my future.

CHAPTER 5
Creating a Counter Culture

Some companies have more than one organisational culture. It requires careful balancing to maintain strong relationships within an organisational unit and across while remaining committed to the organisation's overarching aims. Sometimes you may drop the ball. The trick is to maintain your integrity.

THE GED-ITES

In addition to leading electrical buying for Courts Singapore, I wore a second professional 'hat' at Courts as head of the regional buying team under Ged Dempsey. Courts had just designated Singapore as one of two regional buying centres. They had established a Miami centre to serve Caribbean markets, which quickly made a huge impact on the profitability of the electricals business in the region. In Singapore, we were a bit slower getting off the ground for reasons that I will describe later, but we achieved some limited success.

My role in the regional buying team created another source of tension between Albert and me for two reasons. The position gave me a dotted line both to London and to the other buyers in the region, which meant that I didn't need Albert's approval regarding regional buying decisions. In addition, Albert considered me to be his staff and didn't want anyone else drawing on his resources, so every time Ged wanted me to participate in a team meeting, he'd first have to ask Albert for permission for me to join in.

I suppose that this illustrates one of the downsides of the Courts model at the time. On the one hand, I think that Courts' decentralised structure worked well in that it gave individual countries considerable leeway to operate in the manner that they felt was best suited to the local markets. On the other hand, it seemed to me that some individual country-managing directors viewed their markets somewhat as personal fiefdoms. They therefore resisted any action seen as encroaching on their autonomy—such as the regional buying initiative, or in my case, the way that the regional buying role gave me a connection to London that bypassed Albert.

At the start, the regional buying opportunity in Asia wasn't that big since a lot of the brands did not operate at the regional level. For example, Sony Singapore didn't talk to Sony Malaysia, so there wasn't much point in trying to aggregate our buying, since there was no regional Sony entity to approach. I thought there was actually more to be gained by eliminating distributors and setting up direct accounts with suppliers—which we did—but there was less of an opportunity to amalgamate product and delivery centrally.

Despite this, we continued to work on attaining whatever synergies and economies of scale that we could. While centralised regional buying did not really work for Singapore and Malaysia, we did make significant improvements in these two markets in local terms, such as through the bypassing of distributors. And by centralising regional buying and product warehousing, we boosted the performance in smaller Courts markets such as Fiji, Mauritius and Papua New Guinea.

My role as regional buyer was a source of tension between Albert and me. The regional buying team presented a sort of counter-culture to Courts Singapore's operations. Many in London called us the 'Ged-ites', a reference to the justice-serving Jedi warriors in the Star Wars movies. Ged's idea was that our group was going to subtly but positively change Courts' business in Southeast Asia.

I viewed working with regional team members as a form of stress relief. We would have a day or two of meetings that would involve a lot of hard work, but we would also have a bit of fun together, and this helped to keep me happy in the job. I suppose we saw ourselves as the vanguard of a new, sexier side of the business, particularly in contrast to the more staid furniture business. In fact, we had a nickname for the furniture guys, we called them 'Woodentops'.

I learnt a lot from being part of this regional team, especially through my interactions with Ged. He was an excellent manager and ran the team in much the same way that I approach my teams today. I remember that one of his key sayings was, "While I demand your loyalty, I will earn your respect." I saw that Ged took nothing for granted; he had no sense of entitlement. Ged simply worked hard to achieve his goals and led by example, and the rest of the team respected this and followed suit.

The answer's yes, what's the question?

Another saying Ged had was, "The answer's yes, what's the question?" Essentially, the idea was that we were not there to say what couldn't be done. We were there to make things happen. And that's exactly what I set about doing in Singapore, although it was by no means a straightforward process.

BACK TO SCHOOL OR BACK TO THE WALL

Beyond facilitating strong team spirit among regional buyers, Ged was a key supporter of my continuing education. One of my weaknesses (in my opinion) was that I never finished my A Levels—the exams required to gain entrance to university.

One night, when Ged and I were in an Irish bar in Bangsar, in Kuala Lumpur, I told him about leaving school part way through my A Levels. Ironically, Ged responded by suggesting that I do an MBA. My first thought was: Don't be ridiculous, I didn't even complete my A Levels and I haven't got a degree, how am I going to do an MBA? However, Ged thought that I would qualify based on professional achievement and other criteria required of mature students. He also mentioned that several other Courts executives had received some company funding for their MBAs. Something about Ged's 'why not?' approach resonated, and I decided to look into it.

I approached the University of Stirling—it has a relationship with the Singapore Retailers Association—and I spoke with a professor whom I'm still in touch with today, Dr Paul Freathy. We sat down for half an hour and at the end of our chat he said he thought my application would probably get through if I wanted to go for it. By now I was pretty excited about the idea, so I decided to bring it up with Albert.

When I told Albert I wanted to do an MBA, his instant reaction was no, you're not doing an MBA. I imagine that he was concerned about the costs involved. I told him that there was a company scheme where the company would pay 50 per cent and the individual pays 50 per cent, and that a few of our managing directors had already done this. But Albert was adamant and simply said that, as Courts didn't pay for his education, they wouldn't pay for mine.

Meanwhile, at the head office in London, Ged had asked our CEO Bruce Cohen to discuss the MBA with me. So Bruce called me and said that they would be happy to pay 50 per cent of my MBA fees. However, he asked me to send the bill directly to the London office—that there was no need for Albert to know. Though it was good for me, this approach epitomised the inherent weakness of the Group's management style: instead of taking Albert to task and telling him what the company's approach to education was, they wanted to avoid confrontation and smooth things over. To be sure, Bruce's action reflected his desire to manage relationships in a way that kept everyone in the company happy. Sometimes, though, it just made things worse.

Things came to a head when Albert inadvertently discovered about my studies in 1996, two years after I had been enrolled in the MBA (which I'd been doing on my own time). The fees for the MBA were paid over three instalments, with London paying the first one, me paying the second one, and the third one was split 50-50. Everything went well until the third bill came in—bear in mind that there was a gap between the first and the third bill of two years, meaning plenty of time for accounts staff to change, knowledge of arrangements to change, etc. Unfortunately, someone in London picked up the bill and saw Singapore on it, and thus sent it over to our office where it landed on Albert's desk. As you might guess, Albert was less than pleased.

Albert called me up one day and told me he had a bill in his hand from the University of Stirling, and that he'd like to speak to me about it. That was the first time in my career that I went to my boss' office expecting to lose my job.

When I got there, Albert indeed accused me of going behind his back. I replied that I was simply taking advantage of a scheme offered by the company, and that he had no right to deny me that. Albert felt he should fire me and I told him I was ready to accept that if that was his decision. He said his instincts were to cancel my work permit, but he would take a weekend to mull it over. You might imagine how anxious I was to get an answer on Monday morning, but I had to wait until the afternoon for Albert to summon me to his office. I spent half the day kept in suspense about the fate of my job. Fortunately, he had decided to keep me on.

LESSON

In the process, I learned another, valuable lesson: **Network up and across your organisation as extensively as possible.** It helps to get to know a variety of senior people in your company so that they are aware of your talent and capabilities and will have you on their radar for new opportunities. (Such relationships can also be an excellent channel for learning via mentorship) I want to stress that I am *not* advocating engaging in office politics—as I wrote earlier in the book, this is something that I detest. While I encourage you to build relationships with senior leaders in your company, this should be done in a transparent and professional manner, not through politicking or stepping on the toes of others.

CHANGES AT THE TOP

One reason why Albert might have kept me was that, despite these issues, Courts Singapore was posting strong results. I had settled into as much of a rhythm as was possible given the need to work under—and around—Albert, and the buying team was doing well. Still, I felt restless. I had promised to work for three years and I had done three years. I felt that while working with Albert was good for me in some respects, I needed to be in a different environment. You can't keep having to massage and manoeuvre just to get the right things done. In the middle of 1996 and the end of my third year with Courts, I submitted a resignation letter to the UK. I told Courts I was open to other offers for jobs within the company, but that I was looking to move on from Courts Singapore. In fact, I was planning to return to the UK to look for a job.

I was a bit anxious about having to find a new job given that I had a family to provide for and no clear idea of what the future held. At the same time, I was only 28 and I wasn't thinking too much about the consequences. I'd been out of the UK for only three years, so I still had good connections in the market there; they were sufficient, I felt, to be able to land a good position. Janice was also supportive of my decision. And her persistent support, of course, has been critical to my success.

> **LESSON**
>
> **Continuously engage your spouse or partner in your career choices.** Careers inevitably affect your personal life, and I know that I am happiest in my work when things are happy at home. It is crucial to involve your partner when making career-related decisions. If a new career opportunity involves moving or frequent travel, for example, you need to ensure that you and your partner are on the same page in terms of hopes and expectations.

However, almost immediately after submitting my letter, I got a phone call from Bruce Cohen. He told me that Courts was making some management changes in the region, including shifting Albert to Malaysia and Bryan Brooks, the managing director of the Malaysia business, to Singapore. He told me that Bryan had a high regard for me and that he thought it would be good for my career to stay on and work with him.

I already knew Bryan at that point, having had some interactions with him through my regional buying role. He was around 60 at the time and was getting towards the end of his career. The indication from Bruce was that Bryan would be retiring within a few years, but there was no promise of his job then going to me. I mulled this over and eventually agreed to stay on, reasoning that under new leadership, there might be opportunity for a new career track. I carried this sense of optimism into my personal life as well, where changes were occurring that would influence my role in both corporate *and* community leadership.

CHAPTER 6

The Non-Linear Path to the Top

Building a career is not a linear path, and opportunities to accelerate your learning as a leader can often be found outside the office. Taking on responsibilities and embracing the chance to make a difference can be both personally fulfilling and contribute to your professional development.

When we first arrived in Singapore, we rented an apartment in Cashew Heights in Singapore's Upper Bukit Timah neighbourhood. We didn't really have a good picture of Singapore before we came, so we were expecting something similar to Hong Kong in terms of cramped living conditions. Hong Kong, as you probably know, is one of the most densely populated cities in the world. We were happy to find quite the opposite in Singapore: we had a reasonably sized apartment in a complex that offered tennis courts and a swimming pool! Janice's mother lived with us at that time, so we had a live-in babysitter for Daniel, who was 17 months when we first got to Singapore, as well as a full-time domestic helper.

All in all, this made for quite a comfortable lifestyle, although work was incredibly intense those first couple of years. While I couldn't have asked for more in terms of a loving family, I felt that there was still something missing, and that was a set of close friends. In Liverpool, I had always had my mates around and we would see each other all the time. In Singapore, my life consisted of work, work, work, and home and baby.

Janice suggested that I should start playing snooker again. The lads and I used to go out to a snooker club on Sunday nights in Liverpool and there was a snooker room at the British Club, where we were members. Thus began my back-door entry into Singapore community engagement.

A SHAKE UP AT ONE OF SINGAPORE'S MORE VENERABLE INSTITUTIONS: THE BRITISH CLUB

Every Wednesday night was snooker night at the British Club, so taking Janice's advice, I walked into the club one

Wednesday and asked the receptionist for directions to find the snooker room. Just then a guy who had walked in behind me—his name was Andy and he was from the Isle of Man, not far from Liverpool—said he would show me the way. It turned out that he was the club's snooker convenor. He introduced me to the lads, and I passed an enjoyable evening. I played a couple games, had a beer, and returned home by 9pm. I went back the following week, played a few more frames of snooker, drank one or two more beers, and got back around 10pm. Fast forward about six weeks and it was a lot of frames of snooker, quite a few beers and a late-night supper afterwards at Adam Road Food Centre.

I was really enjoying those snooker nights and making some good friends among both locals and expatriates. One of the things I like about the club is that it isn't an exclusively expat environment. When I arrived in Singapore, I noticed that expatriates and Singaporeans seemed to socialise in separate spheres. The Club was different, and it has remained so. (I should add that, these days, I find the expat-Singaporean gap to be shrinking.) In such an amiable environment I became so involved in those snooker evenings that when Andy returned to the UK for work, the other guys suggested that I take over as convener. I agreed, thinking there wasn't much to organising the tournaments and annual dinner and making sure we kept the accounts for the Wednesday night beer.

But one thing led to another, and somehow I was asked to join not just the club's sports committee, but also the club's main committee. A number of the guys in the snooker section were quite involved—one in particular, Roger Davis, was bidding for the club presidency. In the end, they succeeded, and I ran for and won a seat on the main committee.

My portfolio on the main committee was sports, so I got to see how each of the sports sections at the club was organised. I may have been biased, but I found that snooker was the most organised section. It had proper funding, proper member participation and well-planned events. A lot of the other groups were much more informal in the way they operated, so I set about reorganising them based on what had worked well for the snooker group. In some ways this was similar to what I was doing with the electrical buying team at Courts at the time: putting in place more organised structures and procedures, building a team of capable individuals empowered to carry out their respective responsibilities, and encouraging a stronger team spirit.

After a while, I had things running quite nicely in the sports section. This prompted Roger to ask that I take on the club development portfolio the following year. I told him I didn't know a thing about development, and that I was no contractor. He said it didn't matter, that I got things done, and that he wanted me on development.

So I moved on to development in 1996/1997. During that period we carried out various projects, including renovating the pool, updating the gym and polling the club's members on development issues. By 1998, Roger asked me to be his vice president. In my view, you become a vice president for one of two reasons: either you view the job as a pathway to the presidency, or you're an effective executioner keen to support the President and the team. I aspired to both roles and fortunately, circumstances allowed me to realise this ambition earlier than I had thought possible. As it turned out, Roger had a lot on his plate that year as he was changing careers and starting up his own company. Since he couldn't make a lot of the meetings, I ended up chairing a lot of them that year.

One of the reasons I was able to scale up my responsibilities at the club is that its facilities allowed me to integrate family, work and social activities. Janice and I welcomed our daughter, Jennifer, to the world in 1995—just when I was steaming ahead with activities at Courts and the British Club. Jennifer could play in the club's childcare area while I attended meetings, and Daniel and Janice could make use of the other recreational facilities if I was working. I never felt like I was spending time away from my family.

Consequently, when Roger announced that he was moving to Taipei in 1999, I asked a few of the more experienced committee members if I should stand for the presidency, and I gathered a good bit of support. Bear in mind that in 1998 I was 30 years young; back then, most club presidents were at least 50. To be honest, I think that's what attracted me to the position. It was an opportunity to change some things, to shake things up.

Although I certainly had more than enough going on at work to keep me busy, I was drawn to the prospect of running for president of the British Club because it presented an exciting challenge in change management. I saw that while many things were done very well at the club, there was also significant potential to bring about meaningful improvements. I also believed that the club offered me a chance to practise some of my developing business skills.

In addition to what I was learning at Courts, my MBA studies equipped me with a set of skills that I thought I could make good use of at the club even though I was by far one of the youngest members on the Executive Committee. Until the mid-1990s, for instance, the club had operated without a strategy. It offered no mission statement, no set of core values, and, until then, no strategic development plans.

With that in mind, one of my principal acts as vice president was to call an offsite strategy meeting to map out the club's future. I remember spending much of the meeting convincing members of the need for a strategy meeting: our members' expectations were changing and the competitive landscape among Singapore clubs was changing, and I thought that the club needed to actively respond to these changes.

I won the presidency in 1999 and held the position until 2002. By the end of this period, I felt I had been able to make a positive impact and was happy to hand over the reins to someone else. In retrospect, I feel that three years is the ideal length for a president to hold office in this type of voluntary environment: one year to assess, one year to implement and one year to hand over. Over the course of my three-year term, we reorganised management to place greater emphasis on marketing and membership; we implemented a leadership training and development program; and we executed many infrastructural upgrades.

While serving the British Club, we'd often work with most other British community organisations around town, such as the Chamber of Commerce. So it should have come as no surprise that, just when I was stepping down as President of the British Club, one of my contacts at the British Chamber of Commerce suggested that I get involved with the Chamber.

Trouble was, I had already told Janice that I was stepping down to spend more time with the family. But my friend suggested that I wouldn't need to supervise any committees or projects, I'd just have to go to a monthly board meeting. Knowing me, I should have known better.

It wasn't long before my friend, Shankar, at the British Chamber, asked me to take over chairing the group's 50th anniversary committee, which was planning a huge golf tournament. I said, "Shankar, you said just a few months ago that I don't need to do anything." He replied, "Yes, I know, but the anniversary committee chairman is leaving Singapore and we figure that your British Club experience would make you a great shoo-in." So I agreed, figuring that, as late in the year as it was, the party would have been already well-prepared.

The reality was that the anniversary committee had yet to nail down a plan. When I found out, I thought, 'ok, fine, basically said there's only one thing that we can do with this much notice: the simplest thing to do is to take everything that we already do and put it on steroids. We don't need to think of too many new things, but let's just take what we do and double it.'

So instead of one golf tournament we'd have two. And we'd have a British Business Awards event. Basically, we just went through the programme for the year and said bigger, better, more dynamic, wider scope, more partners, et cetera. It was the same principle that I applied to my service at the British Club, and with Courts.

To kick it off, I even suggested that we take a punt and invite Lee Kuan Yew to attend our gala dinner as guest-of-honour to kick off the year. We asked the High Commissioner to extend the invitation to him, and we got a positive response. In the end about 850 people attended the event—the biggest event ever held by the British Chamber of Commerce.

It was 2004, and it had been a good year, and I went naturally from that into chairing the Chamber's Events committee. A year later, I began working with the Chamber President Jonathan Asherson as vice-president. It was an amazing experience, hosting and entertaining dignitaries such as Tony and Cherie Blair, John Major,

David Beckham, Posh Spice, several British Olympians—and Her Majesty, The Queen.

By 2006, Jonathan was stepping aside and I felt game to continue my work there, and made a successful bid for the Presidency. It was difficult to take on the chamber the year after hosting the Queen. You can't get much more excitement than that. But I realised that it wasn't going to be a single event or any showmanship or anything like that that was going to define my presidency. Thinking strategically, I realised that the one thing the Chamber is supposed to do is to provide networking opportunities. So I made a simple, tactical decision: I decided to grow the membership.

But first, I had to assemble a team. To grow the membership, we needed to get closer to our membership, to segment it the right way, understand what they want, understand what they want to network on, understand what kind of topics they want to listen to, what kind of speakers they want and so on.

Unlike the British Club where you have 120 staff, at the chamber you're looking at five or six staff. You might have hundreds of members, but the infrastructure is quite limited, so we really need top-flight people in that small group. I recruited an executive director and went to the board and said, right, I've got the new executive director.

They're like, right, ok, who is he? Well, first of all, it's not a he, it's a she. And secondly, she's not British, she's German. There were some looks around the table at first, but they got used to it very quickly, and Brigitte Holtschneider is still the executive director of the chamber and is doing a great job.

The mantra was very simple: bigger, closer, smarter. We need to grow this thing to the maximum number of members we can grow, not only in terms of the number of companies, but also in terms of the nominees within each company so that there's a bigger community. We need to segment the membership in a smarter way. We need to make sure that we are well specialised within those segmented groups. And we need to be smarter by having more content, participating in pre-budget discussions, networking with other chambers, and learning from the best about what they do and then importing it.

We tripled the membership and doubled the cash reserves over a four-year period. We also became more visible in the community and focused on branding. I reply to a *Business Times* column called "Views from the Top" from time to time. When I did so at that time, I would sometimes reply as CEO of Courts, President of the British Chamber of Commerce, and other times as President of the British

Chamber of Commerce, CEO of Courts. But I always replied double-barrelled so that both Courts and the chamber would gain exposure and piggyback on one another.

During that time I also built strong relationships with the British High Commission. I was supposed to step down in 2009. I had set exactly the same timeframe as I had at the British Club, so I'd said that I would stay with the chamber as president from 2006 to 2009. In 2009, I had a conversation with Amanda Brooks, the Deputy High Commissioner—she's the head of UK trade and investment and sits on the chamber's board. I said to her, "Amanda, do you think it's ok for me to step down?" We were basically still in the mire of the global financial crisis, so I would have stepped down in May 2009, but I was really asking the question in early 2009, so it was really right in the middle of the shit. I felt like the chamber was in great shape, but that I'd be walking away and potentially be leaving a mess if things got worse.

Amanda said, "I don't think he—then High Commissioner Paul Madden—will mind, I don't think he'll have a view either way. He's the patron of the chamber, but the chamber determines itself how it wants to run." However, a bit later she came back to me and said, "Well, he feels pretty strongly that it would probably be a bad sign for the president to step down right now, just for continuity sake given the fact that there is an external crisis on at the moment." So I took that view on board and decided to stay on for another year. I consulted the board and said that I would extend my time as president by a year, so I did that and stepped down in May 2010. I wanted to stay on for the health of the chamber, but I also didn't want to overstay my welcome.

In late May, early June 2010, my PA Ada got a phone call and passed on the message to me that the High Commissioner wanted to see me. I asked, "Why, what have I done?" She said, "I don't know, but they want to see you between 11am and 2pm today". So I said 'ok' and drove over there. As I was sitting in the reception, the High Commissioner walked past and didn't say a word, so I was thinking, 'Oh shit, I've upset him or something.' It turns out he just didn't see me, but he then doubled back and said, "Oh Terry, come in, come in." So I went into his office and he asked how my family was. After chatting for a couple minutes I asked him, "Paul, why am I here?" He said, "I'll get to the point. I'm delighted to inform you that Her Majesty, The Queen has decided to bestow upon you The Most Excellent Order of the British Empire."

I was stunned! It's funny, because when you're the most stunned you say the most stupid things. So at that moment, all I could think to say was, "Wow, thanks!" I drove straight home and told Janice. I got quite emotional thinking about my dad, who had passed away in 2001 and wasn't around to see this. I wish that he had been there to share this with me.

As you'll read next, my British Club and Chamber of Commerce experiences paralleled what was happening around the same time with my role at Courts. In hindsight, the dual roles seemed to work in synergistic fashion: I found the kind of tactics that I used to win support for the Club presidency and help implement the Board's strategic agenda to serve equally well at Courts and, later, when I served as President to the British Chamber of Commerce from 2006 to 2010. One of these tactics is to know how to be a productive apprentice. I've always believed that one of the keys is to be a really good number two—in fact the primary role of a number two is to make the number one guy look good. I approached working with Roger at the British Club in the same way that I worked with Bryan Brooks at Courts.

NEW LEADERSHIP

Bryan's arrival as managing director of Courts Singapore in 1996 marked a huge change for the business and for me personally. Bryan and I instantly hit it off, and I really took to his style of management: very empowering and very personable. Like Neville, Bryan became a guide to me. But, whereas Neville was like a father who pushes and pushes you until you make a breakthrough achievement, Bryan was more like a mentor proud and supportive of his prodigy's achievements.

Originally from the UK but an Australian citizen, Bryan had run the Courts business in Australia and Fiji before establishing Courts' Malaysia business in 1987 and continuing to grow it until his move to Singapore. When he arrived, Bryan was planning to work for two more years and then retire in 1998. At the time, I already felt that I could and should be his successor. I'm not sure whether Bryan saw it that way at the start, since we had never worked together before. But I spent the following years working hard to prove that I was the right person for the job. Over time, Bryan came to agree. A year after arriving, Bryan promoted me to the role of Commercial Director. This was probably a more accurate reflection of what I was doing at the time. The role essentially

Bryan Brooks at the opening of the Malaysia store in 1987.

encompassed electrical buying, the new IT category, as well as marketing, customer service and basically all other commercial functions except furniture buying.

UNLEASHED

Nevertheless, this move marked a new turn for both me and for Courts Singapore. Under Albert, the organisational culture at Courts Singapore was relatively conservative. I didn't feel that I could fully run with my ideas and vision for the business. Bryan brought a style of management to the table that enabled me to implement some of the changes I'd been keen to make, such as investing more heavily in people, service and new products.

For example, until Bryan's came on board, we had no formal customer service function. Sure, we had a department that was called Customer Service, but to me it was just a complaints department. What I wanted was a department that would look at what we were offering the customer—what's the customer promise, how are we developing the promise, etc. So within a short time of Bryan taking the helm, we created a customer service senior leadership position to strengthen our efforts in this area. We also hadn't invested enough in our warehouses. Following Bryan's arrival we hired a warehouse controller, installed modern racking into our warehouses for the first time, and invested in reach trucks and modern handling equipment.

There were so many things that needed to change to become a world-class business. And they weren't necessarily the low-hanging fruit, like changing the stores and improving the product ranges and those sorts of things. We were looking at processes, structures and back-office aspects of the business. We also wanted to work on things like branding, store design, road shows, and so on. One of the most significant changes that we introduced during that period was the rebranding and repackaging of our credit offer, which we re-launched in October 1996. Soon afterwards, we doubled the previous weekly sales record for our electrical business.

GOING LOCAL—AND GOING ELECTRIC

The culture of the business was also something that needed to be addressed. It was then still very expat-centric, yet some of our brightest people were locals. One watershed moment brought the problem of this cultural gap to the fore.

At one of our first strategy meetings after Bryan arrived, I put the issue of Courts' business culture on the table. Kevin, our furniture director, said it was fine. The other expats also said it was fine. I then turned to Kee Kim Eng, who was then our local Singapore finance director, and asked her what she thought. With tears in her eyes, she said things were definitely not fine. She described a culture of non-inclusiveness, lack of sharing between expats and locals, and a colonial mindset. A lot of this was a result of an old-school management style that didn't pay much attention to the views of local employees—perhaps an unfortunate holdover from Courts' long history as a British company sending Western managers abroad to run its overseas businesses. Kim brought up differences in benefits and a whole range of other issues. Bryan was shocked, and set about looking at solutions.

This ushered in a number of important cultural changes to the Courts business in Singapore. For instance, we made a shift towards having a more equal and balanced management team. We recruited a customer service controller, Kiran Kaur (she is now our human resources director). Kee Kim Eng quickly enhanced her position as finance director by performing critical, strategic analysis—a move that I believe came about in large part to the change in company culture.

> **I won't claim that moving into IT was a stroke of genius on my part.**

Another issue was the 'silo' thinking that perforated the business. Up to that time, we had people who were protecting their own areas and not sharing information and knowledge. I also felt that the culture of the management was a bit too centred on the expatriates, but some of our best people were locals. So I worked with Bryan and the team to encourage more open dialogue. For instance, we asked the more guarded employees to present at our next strategy session, putting them on the spot as it were. It was my job to implement a Courts-wide cultural change.

To do this, we had our first management off-site meeting at a hotel on Sentosa, where the focus was very much on fostering a team spirit and encouraging a sense that we were all working towards a common goal.

Once people saw that we were not out for their job or to criticise them, they realised the value in sharing. People felt more empowered to speak up about opportunities that they saw and areas for potential improvement in the business. This really opened up the lines of communication between our store managers and our department heads and senior management team, and it was a huge benefit for the business in terms of being smart, creative and forward thinking in the way we operated.

While all these changes were taking place, some of our team thought it was the right time to move into the information technology (IT) business. I had been interested in IT earlier, but was advised that the business offered only a 10 per cent gross margin. But Bryan supported my effort to push IT and computer retailing to the forefront of our retail business.

I won't claim that moving into IT was a stroke of genius on my part. Most of the ideas that I introduced to the business were already happening internationally, but hadn't yet been introduced in Singapore. However, based on what I was seeing in other markets with regards to IT, I felt we needed to make sure we didn't miss the boat. I still faced some apprehension from Bryan. Personal Computer (PC) retailing wasn't common for electrical retailers at that time—it was more the domain of dedicated IT retailers, such as the small specialty shops in Singapore's Funan Centre and Sim Lim Square. For this reason, I didn't think Bryan would go for investing in a whole new team to drive the IT business—at least not right away—so it made more sense to use existing internal resources to get things started.

I turned to Steve Church, who was managing our Bukit Timah store, to lead our push into IT. Steve had worked at Courts in Singapore from 1992 to 1993, but he had left before I arrived and went to join Courts Papua New Guinea. There he had taken on a bit of an all-round role, including implementing IT systems for the business, before returning to Courts Singapore a few years later.

When I told Steve that I wanted to combine his role of managing the Bukit Timah store with buying for IT, I felt like I was pouring water on a dry plant. Suddenly, Steve was excited to have something he could really sink his teeth into. It was encouraging to see someone who shared my vision for IT and we got things off the ground quickly in a flurry of activity. We took an existing Courts brand that was being used for office furniture in other countries, Courts Workstation, cleaned it up and repurposed it for our needs. In 1997, we launched Courts Workstation in Singapore with the tagline "Computers made affordable" and it quickly became a huge success—within four years it went from 2 per cent of our business to 30 per cent.

In 1998, we used the success of Courts Workstation to brand our electrical business as Courts Powerhouse. This fulfilled a long-standing ambition of mine to break away from the image of being a furniture seller that dabbled in electricals to become a major electrical player. Now, instead of simply having electrical products for sale in our stores, we had a strong, clearly defined brand under which to promote our electrical offering. It turned out to be a good move. It was a heady period.

UNDAUNTED

When I first joined Courts Singapore, we had some relatively strong years, growing from around $72 million in 1992 to $99 million in 1993, $112 million in 1994 and $122 million in 1995. The trouble was that although we were growing, our growth seemed to be tapering off towards the end of Albert's last year. This reinforced my belief that we needed to get a number of new things going.

We introduced a slew of initiatives, including a revamped credit offer and the previously mentioned introduction of the Courts Workstation and Courts Powerhouse brands. And although the first three or four months of 1996 were quite tough, we ended up hitting $152 million that year, and then $180 million in 1997. To a certain extent this strengthened my resolve that I could do Bryan's job, and I think Bryan shared my vision. On a couple of occasions in 1997 and in 1998, Bryan suggested that I should be his successor, although the choice was not really his to make.

When I was back in the UK for meetings in the summer of 1997, I began talking with Courts CEO Bruce Cohen about Bryan's succession. I made it clear that I wanted to be formally recognised as Bryan's number two and become the deputy-managing director. Initially, Bruce responded with a firm 'no'. He explained that if they made me deputy-managing director, I would have an expectation of becoming managing director in Singapore, and they'd already promised that role to somebody else. I didn't know it at the time, but it turned out that the Singapore managing director job was intended for none other than

Albert's son, Nick Elphick, who was then working at Courts Malaysia with Albert.

Undaunted, I told Bruce that I thought he should make me deputy managing director. I summoned up the guts to say that, although I understood that Bruce would assign the managing director role to somebody else after Bryan retired, I felt confident that he would one day appoint me to the role after he witnessed the strong results Bryan and I were producing.

A few months before Bryan's intended retirement date, a fortuitous series of conversations took place. It started with a conversation I had with Bryan in which he told me he was really going to miss working. He had been living overseas and away from his son Jonathan, who lived in Australia, for 12 years. He told me that he wished there was a way he could keep working and still see his son.

Not long after this, Bruce Cohen mentioned to me that it was a shame that Bryan was retiring. I told him I thought so too, particularly as Bryan actually didn't want to stop working. This led to my telling Bruce about how Bryan would ideally like to keep working at Courts Singapore if only he could see his son more often.

I think our conversation planted a seed in Bruce's head. A few weeks later, Bryan came into my office and told me that Bruce had offered him the option to work 50 per cent of his time in Singapore and the other half in Australia. Bryan had jumped on this offer and agreed to another two years under this arrangement. I later learned that part of the reason Bryan agreed to stay on was to open up an opportunity for me to become managing director upon his retirement. In retrospect, I think that this was one of the nicest things that anyone's ever done for me and my career.

Meanwhile, instead of placing Nick Elphick in Singapore, the Cohens made Nick managing director of Malaysia and appointed Albert as chairman of Courts Malaysia. It was a typical Courts reshuffle that allowed management to avoid confrontation or upset, even though some changes might have been good for the company. But it did give me another two years to prove myself.

It was during these couple of years that our team really came together. We opened new stores in Orchard Road and in Woodlands, in the north of Singapore. We felt a strong sense of ownership in the business because a lot of the concepts that we'd created, we'd created together. We also saw ourselves as very different from Courts UK—a little bit like a maverick—given our emphasis on building up the electrical and IT businesses, while the UK remained steadfastly focused on furniture.

Our Singapore management team was aware that the Cohens were intending to bring in someone new as Bryan's successor as Singapore managing director, and they seemed to take on an almost siege-like mentality. They were very much opposed to the idea of an outsider being parachuted in to take over from Bryan, so they'd frequently ask if they could do anything to help influence the Cohens' decision. While I appreciated the support, I tried to stay removed and would simply reply that whatever happens, it will work out.

This show of support illustrated to me how much our senior management team was starting to gel. Our team included Steve Church, who had immense potential, buying Courts' furniture range (he had made the shift from managing the Bukit Timah store to taking on this role following the departure of the previous furniture buying director); Kiran Kaur, our customer service controller, who later took over warehousing and logistics before settling into her current role as HR director; and Kim, our finance director, who by now was leading our strategy sessions with key insights and analysis. We also made a very fortunate addition by poaching James Friel from Courts Indonesia. He joined us in 1998 as electrical buying director—the best in the entire Courts group, in my opinion—and is still with us today as our COO.

Meanwhile, I kept the marketing team very close to me, partly because marketing has always been my forte, and partly because I knew marketing would be key to Courts' success going forward.

THE MAGIC OF THINKING BIG

The 1999 to 2000 period allowed me to really show my abilities as a leader. While Bryan was still the managing director, the fact that his time was split half-half between Singapore and Australia meant that a lot of the responsibility for the day-to-day running of the business fell to me, and he encouraged me to embrace this opportunity. The result was that during this period the Cohens gradually came to accept that I would make a good successor to Bryan, and about six or seven months before his retirement it was announced that I would be taking over as managing director.

> **I set myself a mental target of age 30 to become a managing director.**

I was thrilled with this decision because I thought it would enable me to drive Courts' business forward in Asia. While the Cohens had previously indicated that I would eventually be given a managing director position in one of the overseas Courts businesses, I had little interest in taking over one of the markets in the Caribbean or elsewhere. I felt that Singapore offered one of Courts' most dynamic and challenging competitive environment. And since I was part of a dedicated and cohesive team in Singapore, I did not want to leave.

On a personal level, my appointment as managing director fulfilled a goal that I had set several years earlier. I recall expressing a desire to be a chief executive as early as 1989. I was attending a consumer electronics show in Chicago with Neville Michaelson, the chairman of Colorvision, and over lunch in one of the exhibition halls, we talked about the running of Colorvision and the different roles of the chief executive and chairman.

The way Neville talked about running Colorvision reflected his belief in the principles expounded in David P. Schwartz's book *The Magic of Thinking Big*. The basic idea is that if you set your goals high and acquire the knowledge and ability to achieve them, you will. By the end of our talk, I came away with the idea that I wanted to become a CEO someday. I read the book at Neville's recommendation, and years later it inspired me to name meeting rooms at Courts Headquarters after traits that are essential to achieving goals.

I started to see the potential of turning this somewhat vague goal into reality once I joined Courts. As I assessed where I fit in the management of Courts Singapore and what I had to offer the business, I became more confident that I had the skills and leadership abilities to run a company. I then set myself a mental target of age 30 to become a managing director. While technically I became managing director only in mid-2000 at the age of 32, I felt that I had effectively achieved my goal given that over the previous two years I had been taking a leading role in running the business as deputy managing director. I will always be grateful to Bryan for having stayed on those extra two years, as it provided me with an invaluable opportunity that helped me reach the position I'm in today.

After four years at the helm, Bryan retired in June 2000. We managed to persuade Paul Cohen, our chairman, to come out to Singapore for the retirement party, and we invited all other managing directors from around the region. We had the Flying Dutchman, a local radio deejay, to be the emcee. But most importantly, we invited Jonathan, Bryan's son, who came up from Australia. Bryan didn't know any of this, so it was a huge surprise when we took him to what was supposed to be a quiet dinner at the Grand Hyatt, and suddenly it was a full-on party. Surrounded by good friends and family and with champagne flowing long into the night, it turned into a great send-off. And it marked a new start for me.

CHAPTER 7

Taking Charge

Leaders show their stripes in times of adversity by instilling their teams with a sense of hope, rather than despair. This is when communication skills—or what corporate guidebooks call 'emotional intelligence'—matter most.

Bryan's retirement in June 2000 was an emotional time for me. On the one hand, a great colleague and wonderful friend was to leave Singapore, bringing a slightly bittersweet end to one period of my career. Yet on the other hand, I was brimming with excitement at the prospect of finally being fully in charge of the Singapore business.

When the last of the champagne had been polished off and the farewell party came to a close, I knew one thing for sure: there was plenty to be done.

My very first act on taking over as MD of Courts Singapore in 2000 was to dispense with 'Mr', 'Mrs', 'Boss' or any other hierarchy references among our team. Instead, the management team responded to their given names—'Terry', 'Kim', 'James' and so on. Later, we took a step further and removed offices entirely. I don't have an office and the shift to open plan has helped communication hugely. It was a big sell to my senior team to have them relinquish status symbols but I tried to lead the way by removing my own parking space, by deferring the best parking spaces to customers.

The point of all of this is for senior leadership to not take themselves too seriously and to be approachable. In a modern world you wear your seniority by how you behave not what your business card says or the benefits you have. When staff and colleagues see humility in their leaders, see you pushing yourself out of your comfort zone for them and for customers the bonds across levels get stronger .We renamed our head office as support centre to send out a message that the only reason the office exists is to support the stores who in turn support the customers.

The idea of an inverted pyramid is not new but evidence of companies organising themselves around a customer-centric and non-heirarchical approach seems too rare.

Alongside these strong team-building exercise, Courts enjoyed robust performance during my first couple of years as managing director—but we did make a couple of wrong turns.

Around 2001, I believed—wrongly, it turns out—that with Singapore's market maturing, we should begin exploring entry to markets in the Philippines, Thailand and South Africa. Unfortunately, our forays into South Africa and Thailand were ill fated due to a combination of troubles at home and abroad.

TROUBLE AT THE HEADQUARTERS

At the same time, the Courts UK business was struggling. This had been somewhat common knowledge for a while, and people within Courts knew that the company's debts were going up. UK stores were also coping poorly amidst many new, trendy retailers in the local furniture market. The likes of stores such as Ikea, DFS and Furniture Village targeted specific segments of the UK consumer market, while Courts was still trying to find its niche.

In 2001, James Friel and I, and four other managing directors—Albert Elphick from Malaysia and three managing directors from the Caribbean—were called back to see our chairman, Robert Shrager, to participate in a strategic review. Robert had taken over from Paul Cohen, who had retired earlier that year.

Gathered in a hotel and discussing things over dinner, all six of us had pretty much the same thing to say: Courts should pull out of the UK and focus on the developing markets. We acknowledged that there were obviously strong emotional ties to the UK given the Cohen family connections and Courts' long history, but our UK business model wasn't producing results. Unlike stores in newer markets such as ours, Courts UK didn't move from high street to big-box retailing early enough. They also continued to emphasise furniture sales despite the considerable success Courts stores overseas were having selling electricals. It didn't help that UK management maintained generous but costly benefits for family and long-term employees.

In mid-2002, the company took another series of hits. We were just emerging from the fallout related to the bursting of the dot-com bubble. Not long afterwards, we were dealing with the impact of the severe acute respiratory syndrome (SARS) outbreak, which put a dent in Singapore's economy that year. Singapore started to see unemployment hit 5 per cent, which, while not high by Western standards, represented an unprecedented level of structural unemployment in Singapore. Interestingly, this didn't particularly hit Courts' sales, but it did hurt people's ability to service their credit and make instalment payments. Bad debts slowly started to rise, resulting in a difficult year from mid-2002 to mid-2003.

It was quite a rude wake-up call when I realised that we might have our first-ever loss-making year. During my entire time as buying director, commercial director, deputy managing director and managing director, one thing I wasn't ready for was structural unemployment in Singapore. I'd never dealt with a bad-debt crisis, so I found it quite daunting.

My desire to be pro-customer and pro-community didn't work when it came to collecting debt.

Since I recognised that I lacked the skills or know-how to address the issue, I asked Howard Cohen to recommend the best credit person in the entire Courts group. He suggested Curtis Tobal, who had previously been the credit director at Courts in Trinidad. He had recently been offered to Courts in Malaysia but been turned down by them, which left him looking for a posting within Courts. I jumped on this opportunity and soon had Curtis in Singapore.

Curtis was a large, imposing Trinidadian who, true to his reputation, got things done. I realised that my desire to be pro-customer and pro-community and a bit warm and fuzzy didn't work when it came to collecting debt. Curtis and I agreed that his role was to put in the stricter standards of collections, customer communications and counselling, to get the money owed to us back.

Much as I'd hoped, Curtis came and added rigour to the credit department's operations. He brought forward the collection cycle and he wrote off debts that needed to be written off. Curtis also implemented a policy to charge creditors late payment fees first and principal second. His strategy proved successful, and within a year we were back on track.

...AND ABROAD

While coping with credit issues in Singapore, we were facing even greater challenges in Thailand, where we'd entered the market in 2002 as part of my gung-ho, conquer the world mentality. In Thailand our problem wasn't bad credit or processes, it was the sheer scale of fraud.

Our foray into Thailand had its roots in a stake we took in a business in South Africa with Courts Plc, our parent company. Bear with me now, because I know that South Africa is a long way from Thailand. In 2000, Courts Plc was negotiating a joint venture with South Africa's Profurn to open a store in Johannesburg. The Courts team in the UK thought that the project would benefit from our experience in catering to emerging market customers, so they invited Courts Singapore to take a 25 per cent stake in the venture. I was hopeful that the project would contribute to our growth, but my hope turned to dismay when we arrived in Johannesburg in advance of the first store's opening. I found the store's location in a leafy, well-to-do suburb contrary to Courts' objective to deliver low-priced, affordable, quality goods to an emerging market of middle-class consumers.

Even more dismaying was the fact that just days prior to opening, the store had no merchandising. To help out, our Singapore team rolled up our sleeves to quickly stock the floors, calling on all of Profurn's available merchandising staff. After about an hour, Profurn's staff suddenly disappeared from the floor. Turns out they'd been called away by Profurn's CEO to help out at a cocktail party planned for later that day. Not the most effective use of merchandising staff, if you ask me!

The store did open, but, as I expected, its performance was less than optimal. Meanwhile, Profurn put a freeze on all new projects due to their realisation that they'd overexpanded. At that, we decided to pull out of the venture. Compared to Courts Plc, our other partner in the venture, Courts Singapore got the short end of the stick. We had to write off equity, while Courts Plc swapped some shares in Courts Mauritius with Profurn in return for its JV shares. So it cost Courts Plc nothing and it cost us $3.5 million.

In return for taking a hit in the failed South Africa venture, I persuaded Courts Plc to allow us to enter Thailand. I argued that we had had to pull out of South Africa through no fault of our own because Courts Plc couldn't get on with the partner. Since I had shareholders to answer to, I felt it would be a fair trade-off for Courts Singapore to be given a new territory.

At the time, I viewed Thailand as a logical next step for us in the region. Singapore, Malaysia and Indonesia were taken, so the obvious market was the next biggest one—Thailand. We were looking for a market that was organised in terms of retail, reasonably sophisticated, and within the region, and Thailand seemed to fit the bill.

> **Our credit offices would get phone calls from so-called 'friends' of applicants, threatening staff if they turned down the application.**

But our future problems were probably written from the start. The Group Board didn't want us to go into the capital, Bangkok, because it didn't fit with their vision of being in island communities and smaller cities. With the benefit of hindsight, I now see that I should have pushed harder to go into Bangkok, the most developed market in the country, rather than following the Group norm and opened up stores in the north and south of Thailand. Bangkok would have been a larger volume market and more cash and credit card sales, rather than the high percentage of credit sales we ended up doing in the smaller markets.

We were in Thailand from 2002 to 2007, and at the peak had 10 stores. We made money in 2003 and 2004,

We entered Thailand with a gung ho, conquer-the-world type of attitude. I was obsessed with international expansion.

but things started to go sour in 2005. Our credit offices would get phone calls from so-called 'friends' of applicants, threatening staff if they turned down the application. We also started seeing a sharp rise in the number of fraudulent claims. I'd never encountered such trickiness, and it didn't help that I made some poor people selections going in.

Bear in mind that this was occurring in the wake of the global dot-com bubble and the SARS crisis in Asia. Our Singapore business also hit a speed-bump in 2003, with rising structural unemployment. All this to say that, in some respects, I felt like a deer caught in the headlights. I wasn't used to making mistakes.

In retrospect, I think that the experience stood me in good stead down the road; it made me a tougher and more incisive leader. My perspective changed and I became more willing to close stores and release employees who weren't performing. Ironically, it was a weakness that the Cohen family shared, but never overcame.

NEW PERSPECTIVES, NEW BRANDS, AND NEW BOARDS
Despite the challenging business conditions at this time—or perhaps because we were having a difficult year—our management team embarked on an entirely new strategy

for our Singapore operations: we decided to fully rebrand the company and upgrade our branches. Our thinking was that there was no better time than during a downturn to increase the pace of change and re-engineer parts of the company that could be improved. This process produced the current Courts logo.

We had been dealing with a brand, a delivery and an identity that didn't fit our current customers. We wanted to appeal to a younger audience. Part of the drive stemmed from my frustration that the Courts brand was different in Indonesia, different in the UK, different in the Caribbean. In Malaysia the brand was known as Courts Mammoth, and Indonesia had chevrons through its Courts logo.

I saw Courts Singapore as a maverick, bringing new retail concepts to Asia—and to Courts as a whole.

How can we be one unified company if we look and feel completely different in different parts of the world? On the other hand, because of these differences, we didn't see the need for consistency, and that gave us considerable freedom to do what we felt was best for us. Fortunately, the UK didn't have much of an issue with our rebranding efforts, and Howard Cohen, our consultant director at the time, ended up being very supportive.

To help see through my rebranding plans, I hired Christina Cooper as our first full-fledged marketing director in 2003. She previously worked for Asda Wal-Mart in the UK and brought with her a track record of getting things done. Christina and I set out with an ambitious objective: to overhaul everything and reinvent the business' identity in a project that we called New Courts.

SHAKING UP THE BOARDROOM

Meanwhile, major changes were taking place in the UK that would ultimately impact our business.

In late 2003 and into 2004, the syndicate of UK banks that had extended debt financing to Courts was growing impatient with the lack of improvement in Courts Plc's performance. Amidst the resignations of several Courts

UK executives, Leo McKee, an experienced and well-known retail executive in UK corporate circles, took over as chairman, thus signaling the end of the Cohen family's position at the company helm.

I guess you'd call Leo something of a heavy hitter. He'd previously served as chief executive of Woolworths in the UK, and had held board positions with Kingfisher companies. Interestingly, he is also trained as a behavioural psychologist. Prior to his arrival, I had to some extent run out of people in the Courts group whom I looked up to as business mentors, so with Leo I thought, 'great, here's a guy who I can learn from again.'

That said, my first meeting with Leo as Chairman—at 6am following a night of clubbing in Las Vegas—wasn't so auspicious. Leo had called a strategic review of the group's marketing and branding in Las Vegas. Christina Cooper, Kiran Kaur, who was running our warehouse and logistics, Steve Church, our commercial director in Thailand, and I arrived early in Vegas on a Saturday night. Since our first official meeting wasn't until Sunday evening, and it was Christina and Kiran's first time there, we went out and had a meal at one of the big-name hotels, and then we went clubbing. We then ended up at the tables in one of the casinos. When all was said and done, we got back to our hotel around 4am with a fair number of drinks under our belts. I didn't feel like sleeping, so I decided to go down and get some breakfast.

WHAT (NOT) TO DO WHEN THE BOSS GIVES YOU A WAKE-UP CALL!

The gods were not smiling on me that morning. I was sitting at my table, feeling the worse for wear, and certainly not up for a meeting with the boss. And whom did I run into? Howard Cohen. He invited me to his table to meet the entire marketing team, including Leo! Now I was still coherent enough to know that I was not in any kind of shape to be meeting my new chairman, but I couldn't think of an easy way to get out of it.

So over I went to join Howard, Leo and the team. Leo explained that they had arrived early to start the marketing workshop. He suggested that since Christina was already in town, she should join them for breakfast to discuss marketing. Now a brief breakfast chat I could pull off, but I wasn't about to put Christina in front of the whole team on an hour's sleep. I told Leo I thought she needed some rest after the long flight over and that she would join us this evening as scheduled. Leo clearly wasn't happy with this, but I stuck to my guns, however wobbly they might have been. Thankfully he didn't push too hard, and after a few minutes I was able to excuse myself and totter up to my room to recover.

That evening, Christina, Steve and I went to meet the rest of the Courts team for cocktails. I hadn't told Christina about my run-in with Howard and Leo that morning, so I cringed when, upon introducing herself to Leo, she told him how we had been out clubbing until the wee hours of the morning! All I could do was listen and think to myself that this wasn't going well. As the evening progressed and Leo worked his way around the room, I got the sense that he wasn't particularly happy with the Singapore team—understandable given that he now knew why I'd kept Christina out of the early meeting! When he finally reached our group, he suggested that Steve should switch from the managing directors' group to the marketing group for the meetings. I was grooming Steve to become the general manager in Thailand, so I didn't agree and I said so. This didn't go over well, and in a tone that was clearly meant to put me in my place, Leo said he wanted Steve in the marketing group.

A few minutes later, Leo pulled me aside and gave me a bit of a lecture about not disagreeing with him in public.

Being a trained coach and counsellor, Leo diplomatically suggested that my method of disagreeing in an open meeting could be disempowering, and gave me a couple of pointers on how better to express dissent. I felt that I needed to do something to get back on a bit of even footing, so I launched into what could be viewed as a somewhat aggressive act of showmanship in my team's defence.

I said to Leo: "I think we probably got off to a bad start and your view of me and my team is probably coloured by the fact that we arrived early and had a bit of fun last night. But why don't you hold your opinion and let me know what you think of us at the end of this conference. I think you'll see that this is part of our work hard, play hard attitude."

I think you'll see that this is part of our work hard, play hard attitude.

He took this well enough, and we left it at that. Then the conference got going and I felt that we presented ourselves well. Our team was comfortable talking about marketing, customers and the commercial side of the business in sophisticated terms. We knew our numbers, knew how to measure performance, and were probably the only ones in the room talking Leo's language. We presented our business plan, our media strategy and our competitive strategy, while one country manager got up and told everyone about some minor store-based events unrelated to strategy. This was the quality gap that I had mentioned to Leo, and I felt he came away with a new appreciation for our team.

I can look back at this as a bit of a parallel to my breakthrough with Neville many years before, when I went off on him and our relationship ended up becoming much stronger. So we had smoothed over the initial bad impressions and I was able to develop an effective and valuable relationship with Leo.

TRYING TO SAVE THE PARENT

Leo and the board of Courts Plc had come up with three flagship projects that they hoped would turn the group around. Our aim was to first restructure the limited companies in the Caribbean, which I think would have returned about US$100 million to Courts Plc. Then, we planned to regionalise the Caribbean and Southeast Asia.

Essentially, they were looking to do transactions and securitisation of receivables books, meaning some heavy financial projects in both the West and the East to return cash to the UK to pay down debt. That was the big plan. It seemed simple enough, but at the same time quite challenging given that five or six of the overseas Courts companies were listed in their own right. This added a layer of complexity that would prove hard to overcome.

Around that time, I suggested that Courts Singapore buy Courts Malaysia. As far back as 2001, when we had our team strategy session, I said that at some point I thought Southeast Asia should be a single business run by a single team. An opportunity came around in 2003, when our bankers introduced us to a company called Roly International. They were a supply chain and sourcing company based in Hong Kong. And they had the Disney and Barbie retail franchises. I believe they were interested in us because they felt that if we combined the Southeast Asian business as one, with them as a major shareholder, they could be our sourcing arm as well. I had a term sheet from Singapore bank, DBS, for around $60 million and a serious intent from Roly to come up with the rest of the money so that Courts Singapore and Roly International could collectively buy Courts Malaysia.

The deal hit a wall when Bruce Cohen dismissed the offer. He reasoned that that since Malaysia was bigger than Singapore and therefore the jewel in the Courts Asia crown, why should we sell it? I explained that since Malaysia's market cap was much higher than ours at the time, this transaction would return the most money to the UK, while unifying the Southeast Asia markets.

I think that Bruce's position reflected the company's general opposition to regional financial management structures—a position that I felt no longer served them. The company operated via independent fiefdoms that until then had allowed each country's management team to adopt the Courts business to individual markets. It also allowed Courts Plc to offer its UK-based senior managers the perk of serving as a 'consulting manager' position to each country, which gave them opportunity to travel to some premium vacation destinations. But times and markets had changed, I thought that, as a single entity, we could take advantage of synergies and cost savings.

When senior management started talking of regionalising the Southeast Asia business in 2004, I jumped on what seemed to be an ideal opportunity to initiate the merger.

When we returned from Vegas, our bankers introduced us to Chris Heine from CVC Capital Partners, a private equity firm. Chris was keen to see if there were opportunities to invest in Courts. Maybe he was aware of the UK situation and the need to pay down debt, or perhaps he saw that Singapore was recovering and that we had returned to profitability. We'd also opened a new store in Toa Payoh, so things were just looking up again. At the same time, we were a young management team and the bankers had suggested that Chris should talk to us and see if there was an opportunity for a partnership.

Over lunch, Chris asked me what would be the five or six things that I would do with this business if I had the funding I needed. We talked about regional synergies, about unifying the brand, and about buying strategy. It was an interesting exercise to think and talk about these possibilities, but in the end I told him that with a new chairman, a new board, and some clear plans to fix the group, I needed to play my part in Courts. I said that if and when the board decides they need to divest Southeast Asia or if something happens that means I'm freer to talk to him, then we could talk again in the future. It was at that point that I really committed myself mentally to helping Leo and the board by playing our part to address the group's issues.

It's important to note that by this time Bruce Cohen had stepped aside as CEO of Courts UK, and Leo McKee—

who supported the idea of regionalising the Singapore and Malaysian businesses—had taken over the role of acting chairman. Albert Elphick also had retired from his position as chairman in Malaysia. If Bruce and Albert had still been at their respective helms, I think the chances of discussions about merging the businesses would have been slim. Albert retired in 2002, and Nick, his son, was still in Malaysia but didn't get the top job. In fact, just before the news broke of Albert's retirement, Bruce called to offer me the post to lead the Malaysia business. I made it very clear that I wasn't interested. I told him if he wanted a managing director for Southeast Asia, then I would consider it, since I thought there was a lot we could do together. But a sideways move wasn't going to happen; I had unfinished business in Singapore, and I wasn't about to leave that to do the same job in a new market. In the end, David Wood, who had been running Courts' much smaller business in Indonesia, took over as the Managing Director of Courts Malaysia.

INTERNAL COMPANY BATTLES: SINGAPORE VERSUS MALAYSIA

In the summer of 2004, David Wood and I were called back to the UK. Courts Plc was at a critical period with the banks and wanted to make sure we were hitting our numbers, as well as get an update on the big financial projects that needed to happen to save the group.

I again brought up the case of Singapore acquiring Malaysia when I was alone with Leo. He could see the advantages of our two businesses combining, but he said Malaysia likely wouldn't go for it. He asked how I felt about being acquired by Malaysia, and I said, "I don't mind. If it comes to the point where these projects are critical to save the group, and I end up out of a job, so be it."

Despite all the work we'd put into Singapore, I decided I was prepared to work towards a regional outcome and a financial outcome that was good for us in Southeast Asia and for the UK, and that would allow us to leverage our synergies and become one business. I felt that the unspoken language was that we just needed to get the deal done and that the management quality in the end would rise to the top.

When we met together—Leo, David and I—Leo let me start with my pitch for Singapore buying Malaysia. Predictably, David's hackles went up and he said there was no way it should happen like that. He argued that Malaysia was bigger than Singapore, and that they should be buying us. I replied simply, "Ok, go ahead."

I was dead serious. I told David that since we are a listed company, so he could form a bid, make an offer, do due diligence, get the corporate line-up sorted out. I said that I couldn't really help as I represent the target company. So, I challenged, "What's your first move? How are we going to do this?"

When we talked about a potential merger between Singapore and Malaysia, we were like two schoolboys in front of a headmaster.

When David expressed some hesitation, Leo told us we needed to work together and make it happen. I pointed out that because I had corporate governance boundaries that I needed to maintain, I obviously couldn't be on the deal team, but I would be happy to sit down with the Malaysia team independently of a transaction and say where I thought the regional synergies and value creation opportunities were. Leo agreed, but David remained unconvinced.

He argued that Singapore and Malaysia shouldn't merge just because the UK had gotten itself in a hole. The thing is, I wanted a merger; I believed in the value of a single company. I believed in a single brand and synergies and that there were operating opportunities. I was operating in a market that was 650 square kilometres and needed territorial, geographical expansion. There's a finite limit to how big Singapore can be. But taking our style of management to another market could bring significant benefits to the business.

Eventually, David agreed to discuss possible synergies. Turns out there were plenty of opportunities. When we started to compare notes, we discovered that, whereas Courts Malaysia paid 5 per cent to Courts Plc's central buying unit for centrally sourced products, we paid only 2.5 per cent. And while Malaysia paid 2.5 per cent of marketing spend to central marketing for the brand, we paid nothing. We also found opportunities to synergise supply terms and rents and in virtually every other area of operating expenditure. Despite the possibilities, weeks went by and nothing happened.

By this time Leo had appointed the company secretary, Chris Lee, as the regional director for Southeast Asia. Chris was therefore my boss, although to be honest the relationship that I had with him was more like mates. Chris was not really a classic commercial guy—as company secretary he was more of a property, contracts and corporate development kind of guy, and definitely not into the sales, commercial, top-line side of the business. This led him to say that I should have a dual role as regional commercial director once we get out the other side of our current problems.

At that point I offered to move to Malaysia, because the only way the transaction was going to happen was if I went there and got it done myself. As it turned out, we never reached that point because things took a turn for the worse back in the UK.

THE UK COLLAPSES

In the second half of 2004, the pressure was clearly mounting on Courts Plc. You could feel the syndicate of UK and overseas banks were growing disenchanted with the business, and were pushing for management changes that, in retrospect, should have been implemented much earlier. We were making absolutely no progress on the limited companies or the regionalisation in the Caribbean. The Jamaican shareholders didn't see the point. And our Southeast Asia plans also stalled.

Leo and the UK team then realised that they needed another 35 million pounds. They were already in debt for 280 million pounds, and with the banks on edge, it turned out to be a tough sell. Courts UK had brought in a turnaround team from Alvarez & Marshal—a global professional services consultancy with expertise in corporate turnarounds—to try to whip the UK business into shape and save it from collapsing. But ultimately this and the other efforts to save Courts Plc were too little, too late given the speed at which the business was unravelling.

In November 2004, the administrators moved in. This was big news in the UK, where Courts was a well-known institution employing hundreds of people.

According to newspaper reports, analysts were taken by surprise by Courts Plc's rapid collapse. Customers and employees also felt the pain. Many customers protested after learning that financial problems meant Courts was unable to complete outstanding furniture orders. (The administrators, KPMG, later arranged to have another furniture company complete orders that had been paid in full). Fourteen hundred employees lost their jobs.

Meanwhile, Courts Singapore became an orphan. We had no parent company. I felt strangely scared and excited at the same time. This was a clear sign that I was at liberty to give Chris Heine at CVC a call. But that wasn't the first thing I did—the first thing I had to do was deal with the fallout of Courts Plc being in administration, and I knew it would take some decisive action to keep things from falling apart in Singapore.

CHAPTER 8

Holding Things Together by Reaching Out

Many leaders advise maintaining a clear boundary between professional and personal lives. I have found that, to the contrary, merging personal and professional interests can, with the right tactics, fuel progress on both fronts.

Maybe it was coincidence, but while I was focusing on holding Courts' business together in Singapore, I was also integrating my personal and charity activities. You'll remember that Uncle John got me involved at age 13 in volunteering at the Northwest Handicapped Children's Society, which he ran with my aunt. The summers that I spent volunteering at the camp for handicapped and underprivileged kids—from age 13 until I left the UK at 24—showed me first-hand what a difference we can make in the lives of others when we make the effort to help, whether this is through donating money, volunteering our time or providing support through other means.

After having been involved in charity work over my 11 working years in England, it felt a bit strange not to be involved in anything when I got here. However, between my new job, my young family and later my responsibilities at the British Club, I didn't have much spare time to focus on other things. As a result, from mid-1993 until 2001, my involvement in charities was limited to things like organising lucky draws at the British Club, providing prizes for charity events or making donations to various causes—in other words, nothing more than what anybody else would do in the normal course of their lives.

All that changed in 2001. By then the kids were a bit older and I was well established in my job as managing director of Courts Singapore. Janice and I were planning a Christmas party at our house in 2001 when a close Singaporean friend of ours passed away from breast cancer. When we heard this sad news, our initial reaction was to cancel the party. But then we thought about it some more and decided to go ahead with the party and make it a fundraiser for the Breast Cancer Foundation.

GIVING BACK

Rather than hosting a regular house party, we charged our friends $50 each at the door as a donation to the cause. We provided food; friends donated booze, and one of the singers from the British Club provided entertainment. With about 80 guests attending, we collected around $4,000 at the door. We also collected quite a bit of money by holding a lucky draw during the party for a number of items signed by Brazilian football legend Pelé that I'd managed to obtain at another event earlier in the year, so by the end of the night we had raised a total of $22,000 to be donated to the Breast Cancer Foundation. Not bad for our first go. And I attribute our success to the strong network we'd built in Singapore over the years.

Unknowingly, we had also thrown the first instalment of what would become an annual charity party—and set in motion a series of events that led to some seriously silly charitable acts on my part.

By 2003, the charity party had evolved into an established annual event significantly larger in scale and ambition than the first one. At this point I decided to get Courts involved in supporting the parties. Contrary to the notion that executives should keep personal and professional lives separate, we found that involving Courts in charitable activities not only served our charitable activities and my personal passion, but also benefited our business. There was already considerable overlap between my personal and business relationships—over the years I had become firm friends with many people whom I first got to know through work—and I recognised that there were plenty of opportunities to make an even bigger charitable impact by getting people and resources from the Courts network involved.

In business circles this is usually called corporate social responsibility, but I just think of it as doing our part to help others. The move towards getting Courts more actively involved in charitable activities was to some extent a natural progression from my own increased involvement in this area.

I consider my wife to be a partner in my career and I frequently use my family as a sounding board for ideas. I also believe that getting the kids involved as volunteers for our charity initiatives and in my work with the British Chamber have helped bring us closer as a family. And I strongly believe that this has contributed to their development into young adults who can hold a conversation confidently with anyone.

By the end of the night we had raised a total of $22,000 to be donated to the Breast Cancer Foundation. Not bad for our first go.

PARTYING FOR A GOOD CAUSE

At our house party in 2001 one of the guests—then Courts' chairwoman of the board, Dr Seet Ai Mee, suggested that we run a similar event for the Dover Park Hospice, which she co-founded. Dover Park Hospice provides care for the terminally ill in Singapore, and we naturally supported its objectives.

After giving it some thought, Janice and I realised that our party had turned out to be quite a good fundraising model, and that we could use it to help other causes. What's more, we had developed quite a wide network of friends and contacts who could contribute the things needed to run a party, and by hosting it at our house there were no venue costs involved. So in the end we agreed to Ai Mee's proposal, and the following year we formed a small committee to organise a fundraising party for Dover Park Hospice. This time we got some other friends involved to help organise things and put in place a bit more proper planning. The result was a party with more than 100 people that raised $56,000 for Dover Park Hospice.

In 2003, we hosted our third charity party, this time raising $63,000 for the Children's Cancer Foundation. This was a tipping point for us, as from that point we embraced the idea that this was no longer an ad hoc event—it was the annual charity house party. And we haven't looked back since then.

From the fourth year onwards, we decided to focus our fundraising efforts on children, and so over the years we've supported groups such as the Straits Times School Pocket Money Fund, Make-A-Wish Foundation, Down Syndrome Association, MILK (Mainly I Love Kids), and Riding for the Disabled Association. For our tenth charity party in 2010 we decided to expand our efforts beyond Singapore, so that year we raised money for a children's surgical centre in Phnom Penh, Cambodia. The number of guests has grown from about 80 at the first party to about 500 at the most recent parties. The amount of money raised has also grown exponentially and is now around $250,000 per party, which allows us to make significant contributions to two or three beneficiaries per year instead of just one.

The organisation of the parties continues to be handled by a small group of friends, family and members of the Courts team. From 2001 to 2007, Janice and I had hosted the parties in the garden at our house. However, in 2007 we moved from a house with a large garden in Brizay Park to our current condominium near Holland Village, and with that we lost the venue for our parties. But with the help of friends and contacts, the parties are still held in low- or no-cost venues.

Organising and running the charity parties in this way has worked out well for all involved. By hosting the parties at a private home, we can avoid the costs involved with paying for a venue such as a hotel. We also work on the basis of getting everything we need to run the parties—food, drinks, sound systems, tentage, etc.—through corporate or personal donations, meaning that there are no operating costs. For example, at the second party in 2002, Janice's friends all donned lingerie and kitchen utensils and did a 'Hey Big Spender' number. My kids have also been involved: at one point Daniel and his friends had formed a band, so they played at a couple of the parties, and Jennifer and her friends have done a few dance numbers. This merger of community and corporate spirit has allowed us to direct every dollar collected from the guests to the party's beneficiaries.

SERIOUSLY SILLY: OR, HOW A LITTLE BIT OF LIVERPOOL GOES A LONG WAY IN SINGAPORE

Of course, we've had to up our game to keep the events interesting. In 2004, our organisers pressured me and a few of my mates into donning tutus and putting on a ballet performance, all in the spirit of 'why not?'. While we were the butt of countless jokes that night, we had a good laugh. At the time, I thought it was a one-off event. But the following year Jennifer said to me, "Daddy, what are you doing this year?" I said, "What do you mean, what am I doing *this year*? I organise this thing. I give away prizes and arm-twist corporates, that's what I do."

Unfortunately, the seed had been planted, and so in 2005, a number of mates and I put on a Bollywood dance routine. Before I knew it, a silly performance became expected every year. And to make matters worse, after

2006, my mates somehow wriggled out of it, which left me on my own to humiliate myself in front of the crowds. Since then I've done everything from "The Evolution of Dance"—the dance routine from a YouTube video that starts in the 1950s and ends up in the present through 33 different dance moves over six minutes—to a hip hop number to a Japanese geisha dance. At some point along the way these became known, quite aptly, as "Moments of Madness". While I was rather nervous before the first couple of performances, since then I've become desensitised, as there's not much that can shock me anymore. And as long as it keeps raising money for good causes, then I'm happy to do it.

We have also enjoyed some very special moments. In 2001, when Courts sponsored Manchester United's tour to Singapore, Jennifer, our then nine-year-old daughter, got to kiss David Beckham. The picture made papers around the world. A few years later, our son Daniel placed himself in the spotlight. Several of my mates visiting from London had been giving Daniel a hard time about his long, unruly hair. At a charity event, he offered them the opportunity to chop it off in return for a donation, setting the minimum at $5,000. In the end, he raised $7,000 for charity and came away with a nice haircut. (In a show of sibling support, our daughter, Jennifer, decided to shave her head, too!)

Bollywood Terry

TACTICAL INTEGRATION OF THE PERSONAL AND THE PROFESSIONAL

Of course, I realised early on that bringing Courts into this mix of personal and extracurricular activities would take some strategising. Since we'd be making use of company resources, I wanted to ensure that this was an initiative aligned with Courts' brand position as a family-oriented retailer. After discussing this with our charity party committee, we decided that going forward the parties would focus on raising funds for local charities whose primary mission was to help children. We then established a hybrid model that aligned our efforts with our personal objectives and Courts' brand objectives. We had also created a model that leveraged both the Courts business network and Janice's and my personal network with the objective of getting everything that we do sponsored.

This took shape in various ways. For example, our shop fitter at Courts helped with providing tentage for the parties, while our media partners helped by providing emcees. My good friend Robert Tham—one of the original members of our charity party committee and owner of an audio supplies business—ensured that our party venues were always fitted out with top-notch audio equipment. Various Courts staff have also been involved in various capacities over the years, helping with everything from marketing and logistics to managing the cashiers and running the auctions on the night itself. We don't really focus on whether it's company or whether it's personal. Instead, we simply focus on getting the best mix of skills and the right mix of contacts in place to get the job done.

In 2006, we flipped things around. Recognising that we had a great team and extensive resources in place to run the annual charity party, we decided to use these same assets to organise a Courts Golf Day for charity. The first Courts Golf Day proved to be a big success, raising about $50,000 for charity, and so this has turned into another annual charity event in which we are involved.

Charity work and a sense of giving have over the years woven themselves firmly into the company culture at Courts, with staff from all parts of the organisation pitching in. Whatever we get involved in, we do our best to run things professionally and we strive to maximise the positive impact of our efforts on society. In some companies I feel that corporate social responsibility can become too political or calculated or complicated, which veers away from the essence of what it should be all about. At the end of the day, all we really should be doing is asking ourselves: What can we do to help others, and why don't we?

CHAPTER 9
Who Needs a Head Office Anyway?

There's nothing like a crisis to spur change.

My first reaction when Courts Plc collapsed in November 2004 was 'Oh shit'.

It felt a bit like being left home alone by your parents and realising that there was no one around to look after you. The flip side of that, of course, was that meant there was no one around to tell us what to do. Or what *not* to do.

Our first task was to engage the media. We were especially concerned about our reputation given what was happening to Courts Plc. The first action the UK administrators, KPMG, took was to close all 88 of the UK Courts stores. A company called Furnitureland negotiated the purchase of six, while the others closed virtually overnight. This caused all sorts of problems for UK customers, because when the administrators moved in they just froze everything—existing orders, warranties, etc. Courts Plc had been ripped apart by UK media for failing to keep contracts with customers. One 2003 headline in *The Telegraph* read: 'Courts receives its sentence of death', with the article going on to describe how tens of thousands of Courts' UK customers protested Courts' failure to deliver the furniture they'd purchased on credit.

The Cohens also came under a lot of criticism—because a few months earlier some had taken their pension scheme early, whereas a lot of employees ended up getting only a fraction of the pension money that they were supposed to.

It was the fastest period in my career in terms of corporate learning.

In the end, Furnitureland made some kind of offer to customers in the UK who had been left high and dry. But the ramifications of the collapse of Courts Plc on the company's pensions and the financial impact on some of the executives went on for a long time.

While Courts' business in Singapore was completely unaffected, I was prepared to be grilled. I called journalists and prepared a press conference to explain in detail that what was happening with Courts' UK business had absolutely no implications for Courts Singapore. We were not financially linked to Courts Plc; we had plenty of cash on our balance sheet because we'd securitised our own receivables; and we were a listed company on the Singapore Exchange with our own board and independent directors. It was true that we expected Courts Plc to sell its 54.16 per cent stake in us, and that would trigger a mandatory general offer, but that was the only implication for our business.

We breathed a sigh of relief when we saw Singapore newspaper headlines the next day delivering the message: 'Courts Singapore Unaffected Despite Parent's Woes'

We were also quick to communicate clearly and openly with our suppliers. Within a week, we managed to get all of our business partners in for a Christmas lunch. Kim stood in front of them and went through our P&L and balance sheet, which showed that we were financially sound. I think there were maybe one or two suppliers to which we made some early payments while they reengineered insurance contracts, but otherwise we continued business as usual.

In the meantime, we had to act quickly to assuage concerns among our staff. We gathered all of our 500 staff together and, backed by the rest of the management team, I explained to everyone that we were going to be ok and asked them not to worry.

A COURTSHIP FOR COURTS

Soon after the implosion of Courts Plc, I called Chris Heine at CVC Capital and said I'd like to pick up the conversation that we'd started the previous year. At that time, I felt wrong about progressing with discussions about a private equity buyout of Courts Singapore when I was supposed to be part of Courts' group turnaround plan, but I obviously didn't feel the same way now. Chris got on a plane and came to Singapore, and we formed a good relationship. Over the course of the following year, CVC very much looked like the frontrunner to buy our business.

But CVC was by no means our only suitor. At the time, 10 or 12 different suitors—some retailers, and some financial institutions—were expressing interest. It seemed like every private equity company and his dog came calling, and some of them were more serious than others.

The process certainly sucked up a lot of my attention and energy. I felt that I was spending more time on corporate finance than I was on retail. Yet it was also a very interesting time because it was by far the fastest period in my career in terms of corporate learning.

At the time I was definitely no expert in corporate finance, so I got a real-time crash course on the topic.

Most investors buying a business don't actually buy companies, they fund management teams.

Fortunately, I had wonderful teachers. I received a lot of input from the KPMG team leading the administration of Courts Plc in the UK, which was led by an Australian woman called Chris Laverty, a real tough nut. I also got a lot of good advice from some of the senior figures in the Courts group, including Leo McKee, the former chairman; Chris Lee, the group's company secretary, who was kept on during the progressive wind-down of Courts' central resources; and Stuart Miller, the group's finance director, who also stayed on for part of the administration period.

I was also learning just by being exposed to lots of banks and private equity funds. And of course I learned a great deal about finance from our Singapore finance director, Kim. In that sense, it was like reverse mentorship.

EXTREME MAKEOVER: RETAIL REVAMPING AND THE OPENING OF THE MEGASTORE

If one of the hallmarks of the period following the collapse of Courts Plc was the 'for sale' feeling as we sat in the shop window, the other was a feeling of liberation. This was a golden opportunity to do things with the business that had not been possible under the Cohens' management. We started with a series of extreme makeovers that had an exponentially positive effect on our business.

For instance, we worked hard to spread the message that Courts is a consumer electronics company first and a furniture company second, partly by renovating every store to lead with consumer electronics. Nobody in the Courts hierarchy had ever accepted that because they had started in furniture.

We certainly weren't behaving like we were facing an uncertain future.

While I was certain that this transformation would strengthen our business, it took us a while to return to the same levels of profitability that we had seen in the late 1990s and early 2000s. Our turnover and our market share were growing, but profits were falling largely because Singaporeans were growing more affluent, which cut into our high-margin credit business. It took us until 2009 to surpass that previous peak level of profitability on a

Singapore basis, although on a group level, with Malaysia's profits added in, we were already miles ahead. But now I'm jumping a bit ahead of my story.

Another major development during that period was that we picked up the pace of discussions with the Singapore government, and specifically the Economic Development Board (EDB), on the possibility of opening a big-box store.

In 2005, the EDB had launched the Warehouse Retail Scheme (WRS). In a nutshell, this was an initiative aimed at supporting large-scale retail businesses in Singapore by encouraging them to bring together warehousing, logistics and related functions under one roof along with a big-box retail component. I saw this as a golden opportunity to be the driver in Singapore's first retail hub, though I also thought it would be beneficial to approach such a large-scale retail development with partners.

Through previous interactions, I knew that IKEA Singapore and Dairy Farm, the parent company of local supermarket chain Giant, were both open to collaboration. We were all in the retail industry serving different parts of the market, so our businesses were complementary. In fact, we had previously discussed possible collaborations in new retail developments, but in the end a decision was made not to participate.

So when EDB launched the WRS, I joined country directors Philip Wee from IKEA and Gary Dunwell from Giant to jointly negotiate WRS terms with the government. Our main concern was that none of the available plots of land under the WRS were suited to our requirements. We all needed something in the east of the country, ideally in the Changi area. We were fine with the location being away from the heart of the city, but it needed to be adjacent to some significant housing and accessible from an expressway. We targeted two major housing developments located at the intersection of two expressways near Changi that were underserved in retail.

The main worry was whether our Courts Singapore team could get the deal over the line quickly. My concern was that if we didn't get this project off the ground before the Courts Plc administration process wrapped up, we would be dealing with a new owner and would likely have to start again from square one with the idea. I had already sold the idea to the UK administrators as adding massive value to the sale of the company—a new $100 million big-box store in the pipeline with huge future earnings potential. We also assured them that it was not going to be too intensive from a capital expenditure perspective because we would get a building lease-back partner. Fortunately, Chris Laverty and her team supported the idea. We also had to get the green light from the independent directors of Courts Singapore.

Following extensive negotiations and planning procedures with EDB, we eventually agreed upon a site in Tampines. A 15-hectare plot of land was designated for a WRS retail hub featuring huge Courts, IKEA and Giant stores, and in November 2005 we held a groundbreaking ceremony with the government. Along with IKEA, we were determined to get our new store—the very first Courts Megastore—open by Christmas 2006. With a huge effort from our team and all of our partners, we pulled it off.

Over the course of that year, I made trips to Chicago and London for layout ideas. I was inspired by the curved glass front of a Crate and Barrel store in Chicago. The glass would allow customers full view of all that we offer, and the curve is considered auspicious in Chinese culture. As we planned the store layout, our megastore somehow morphed from a 54,000-square foot space to 116,000 square feet, in a 280,000-square foot complex. We filled the space with a huge range of electronics organised by category to appeal to a wide customer base. The store allowed us to introduce new branding ideas ('Hot-off-the-docks. From ship-to-shore, you save more') and specialised service areas, such as the 'Doctor Digital' area providing 'technical healthcare'

The glass would allow customers full view of all that we offer, and the curve is considered auspicious in Chinese culture.

services and various 'Countdown Corner' areas featuring time-limited specials throughout the store.

Our opening day was a milestone event for all of us. I remember making a speech on the day of our Megastore opening, and when I finished speaking there was a brief pause, I said thank you, and then every female member of our management team simultaneously broke into tears. I was touched, and felt that this event reflected the sense of achievement we all felt.

Even though these developments took place under the cloud of Courts Plc being in administration, most people in Singapore forgot or ignored that we were majority-owned by a company in administration. We certainly weren't behaving like we were facing an uncertain future. We continued to be accountable to the public as a listed company, and we still had independent directors on board to provide counsel. And from a commercial standpoint, the decisions to reposition our business to electronics-first and to pursue the big-box opportunity were already showing promise.

When it came time to launch the Megastore to the public, we decided to do something big. Apart from the usual sort of promotions, we invited Kelly Rowland from Destiny's Child to give a concert in the car park. It turned

Kelly Rowland at the opening of the Courts Megastore.

out to be a hit, drawing a massive crowd, and I view the whole launch of the Megastore as one of the biggest team achievements in the history of the Courts brand. What's more, the store's sales were huge right from day one. Under the terms of the WRS scheme, we were required to hit $100 million in annual revenue within five years of opening. We had been targeting around $80 million for the first year, but hit $112 million –a game-changing figure, since at that level of turnover, all of our operating ratios looked fantastic.

INSTINCTS AND FLEXIBILITY BUILDING A WINNING TEAM

One of the reasons our business in Singapore was taking off was that we were coming together as a team. We had a strong group of senior managers whom I felt were the right people to take Courts to the next level. Our team included James Friel, who had served with us from 1998 to 2001as electrical buying director, but—at Leo's request—had returned to the UK to assist with the Courts' UK recovery efforts. When the UK business finally went into administration, although I had already filled his position of electrical buying director, I told him to get on a plane to Singapore and we would figure something out to keep him in the Courts' group. I knew he was a valuable asset and well worth having on our team again, so I found a great opportunity to place him in the role of commercial director, overseeing all our buyers and marketers.

Kim, our finance director, continued to be a key resource for the company, effectively serving as Deputy CEO of Singapore as well as Finance Director. And Steve Church, who was getting bogged down in problems beyond his control in Thailand, returned to Singapore to run our furniture and IT buying. I also rehired a woman called Goh Choon Gek, who had worked for me in the 1990s, to take charge of electricals.

Kiran Kaur was another important part of the puzzle. She had started out leading our customer service team, but later moved into warehousing and operations. This may seem like a strange transition, but her customer service role involved her deeply in the logistics side of operations. For example, early on she discovered that we promised customers delivery by 10am, but our trucks left the warehouse only at noon. Kiran consequently worked with the warehousing side of the business to get these kinds of things fixed. These sorts of challenges gave her a well-rounded knowledge of our business, in addition to her keen understanding of our culture and people-oriented values. Given this background, I decided that I would make her our HR director, even though she had no formal HR training. As part of the deal she agreed to do a Masters in HR, which we funded. My instincts proved right: Kiran proved to be a truly top-flight HR leader.

In total, we had a senior management team of about 10. And one of the things I'm most proud of is that during the whole period of administration, we didn't lose anybody. This was a team that went through the fire together and came out the other side that much stronger for it.

Team building has always been a personal passion both at Courts and in my voluntary work. At the heart of it is the 'why are we here' question. Teams operate best when they think of themselves as tribes, as under attack from outside, as collectively trying to scale a new height, turn something around, deliver an item in record quality, speed or both. Shared purpose is a powerful thing.

At the same time, I had benefitted from having Leo around during the period before Courts Plc went into administration. While pleased with the way things were going in Singapore, I felt that my overconfidence in certain situations had produced some mistakes—such as our foray into Thailand—along the way. I respected Leo as a modern retailer, and knew there was much to learn from him. He also added an element of steel in terms of dealing with people issues. Overall, he was good for my personal development and my ability to lead our team and the business.

STEERING AND BEING STEERED

So business was good and the team was coming together, but we still had the fact that we were in the shop window hanging over our heads. KPMG wanted a list of offers from anybody with a pulse, so we were wasting a huge amount of time with people we knew were not credible and were not going to make a bid. That was very frustrating, especially since some of the prospective suitors were our competitors, who were simply fishing for information. However, I eventually realised that most investors buying a business don't actually buy companies, they fund management teams. This helped me to recognise how much decision-making power our group held in deciding who our partner would be.

I realise that this sounds a bit simplistic: there are in fact many instances where people buy companies and kick out the management team. But I felt that our business, being a combination of a retailer and a consumer finance company, wouldn't be so straightforward a purchase. It would be difficult for a retailer to buy our business and understand consumer finance, just as it would be difficult for a consumer finance company to buy our business and understand retail. My gut told me that the likely buyer would be one that bought into the management team and the team's plan. This put me a bit more at ease as we continued to deal with the situation.

At several points in 2005 and 2006, I thought that we were going to sign a deal with CVC. We even got to the point in early 2006 when CVC put in a formal offer. But KPMG rejected the offer as insufficient.

Around that time, KPMG and Stuart Miller, the acting CEO of Courts Plc, were making management changes at Courts Malaysia. They approached me for suggestions on who should take over as managing director in Malaysia, and I recommended James Friel, with the idea of having a friendly face across the causeway. This was a big risk because I didn't know whether the Singapore and Malaysia businesses—still two separate listed companies—would end up being sold together as a regional company, or whether they would be sold in two separate transactions. If the latter occurred, then I had just given away my best guy.

James went up to KL and quickly reorganised the team there. He started with a fresh team including two key members: Chan Yuen Keong, a senior credit manager with an American Express and Citibank background, who was brought in as credit director (he's now based in Singapore as our regional credit director); and Chris Yong from Microsoft, to strengthen the technology business.

By mid-2006, some other serious bidders had also fallen by the wayside. We weren't getting anywhere with CVC; retailers were putting their international expansion plans on hold; other companies we'd scared off with the complexity of our business.. By this time we'd been in the shop window for a year and a half and we were still not sold—our patience was starting to wear thin. But by then, KPMG had already done several transactions for smaller Courts businesses, in addition to the main Courts UK deal, so we were starting to get a little more attention from them.

Finally, in the summer of 2006, KPMG introduced me to Jack Hennessy of Baring Private Equity Asia. After some discussion, I felt that Jack and Baring showed a great deal more financial savvy than the other PE firms. They saw the size and scale of the Malaysian credit book—over the space of a few months, James, Yuen Keong and his team had started to turn things around slightly, so at least from a low point you could see where the business could go. Plus, Malaysia's value had fallen, making it even more attractive.

Another bonus—and a critical one for me—was that the Baring team agreed to let Courts' management continue to steer Courts' course. Some private equity players execute a complete managerial overhaul when they invest in a business, but I think Baring saw that we were very much on the same page as they were with regards to strategy. I'll admit that we spent a few months testing each other's boundaries, such as Baring's consulting with outside advisors on our business. But all that dropped away as frequent and effective communication improved our mutual confidence.

By May 2007, we agreed to a deal. By the time the shareholders were all on board and we had gone through all the mandatory general offers and processes, it was September 2007. It had been a long ride, but the end was clearly in sight, although this time I made sure not to pop the champagne until everything was actually signed!

Looking back at the whole experience, I might describe myself as having been a highly competent retailer in 2000, when I took control of Courts Singapore, but a less than competent corporate operator. I was also a bit self-assured. That gave me something to work towards.

CHAPTER 10
Putting the House in Order

Building winning teams requires letting people go.

After Baring completed its purchase of Courts Singapore and Courts Malaysia in September 2007, we shifted our focus to privatising the Malaysia and Singapore companies. Our new owners recognised that a lot of restructuring would be required to merge the companies' business strategies, and that such transformation would be more easily carried out as a private entity. With that in mind, the company delisted from the Bursa Malaysia stock exchange in October 2007, and completed the privatisation in Singapore in 2009.

In the meantime, I continued in my role as CEO of Courts Singapore and joined the Courts Malaysia board of directors as deputy chairman. This allowed me to play a role in setting the direction of the business in Malaysia. However, since they remained separate companies, I had to be mindful to avoid conflicts of interest.

BLUEPRINT 1.0: THE TURNAROUND PLAN
Management consulting firm Bain & Company played a critical role in guiding each business during this period. Baring had brought in Bain to carry out due diligence prior to their purchase of the two Courts entities. Once the deal was finalised, our joint management team brought Bain back for three months to help develop a strategic blueprint.

I've heard executives complain that management consultants can be overpriced outlets that come in and tell you what you already know. My view is that consultants are a powerful resource if you know how to use them. These firms come with a pool of case studies that can inform business strategy. Plus, they can help point out blind spots. But it's the job of the company's management to guide consultants through the process. There may be tensions along the way. I remember having to intervene when a consultant tried to push an agenda based on another country's market. Using information from outside case studies can be helpful, but using it effectively requires a deep understanding of both the case study market *and* the client's. It's not always an easy task.

Overall, Courts was fortunate to have Suvir Varma lead the Bain team to really understand our business—where it was headed, where it *should* be headed, how best to get there, and so on. Bain recognised that Courts operated two businesses in effect: a retail business and a credit business. This was key, as it helped Baring to see the true value of Courts, and also suggested a path that would lead to a turnaround of the business.

Suvir and his team applied a similarly systematic, data-based approach to assessing our operations, and in that way they added a rigour to the process that Courts would have had difficulty doing alone—even though I felt somewhat vindicated when I saw that their blueprint for how to move forward reflected a lot of what I instinctively felt needed to be done.

Unlike retail shareholders, PE investors focus more on cash flow than on P&L. This enables management to cast off unproductive assets and focus on growing the most profitable elements of the business. Bain refers to this as building 'profit from the core'. That focus enabled us to implement some initiatives that might have been difficult as a listed company. It also helped that Baring had the kind of qualities we were looking for in a partner: a team member that allowed us to be masters of our own destiny, so to speak. I appreciated the fact that none of their suggestions involved me taking my sign off my door and being part of someone else's framework.

One of the core elements of the turnaround blueprint was the accelerated closure of stores in Indonesia and Thailand. The key purpose here was to protect cash: we had clearly gone into these markets too aggressively and we were haemorrhaging cash there. We also had to fix the remaining retail businesses. We went back to basics in a sense, applying some of the classic retail metrics—gross margin per square foot, same-store sales, optimal footprint and the like—to our stores and products.

There were too many different store formats, stores in the wrong places, serving the wrong kinds of customers.

We found that there were too many different store formats, stores located in less-than-ideal places and not serving the right customers. We took a look at how many stores we really needed and what products they should carry. In essence, a complete retail overhaul. In Malaysia this resulted in closing a lot of stores. In Singapore it was about changing the store formats and fully leveraging the success of the Megastore. We also focused on re-energising the sales force by restructuring incentives.

Another aspect of the turnaround was improving our credit business. Here we focused on fixing core processes, approvals and limits. It was also about centralising supply chain operations, particularly in Malaysia, from 23 locations down to one. We zeroed in on quality, reducing bad debts, and running the credit business at low cost.

Lastly, we sought out and drove regional synergies and scale—a theme that I've always believed would play out at some point. This touched on the supply chain, dealing with the brands, renegotiating advertising contracts, and any other facet of the business where we could build scale and find operational or cost advantages. We focused on harnessing the power that we had with suppliers, media owners, etc., and turning it into value for the business.

The details of our results over the past three years are covered in the following chapter, so I'll leave them out here and just reinforce that our strategy has been hugely successful. We've since teamed up with Bain again to look at the next steps for Courts—how we can get from where we are today to being a $1.5 billion business.

A MALAYSIAN MAKEOVER

Soon after joining the Courts Malaysia board, I sat down with James Friel and his Malaysian team to discuss strategy. Together with Bain, we had developed a set of parameters for new store openings that set standards for what a new store should look like in terms of size, scale, format, productivity and so on. After applying these parameters to the Courts Malaysia business, we identified 22 stores that did not meet the requirements; collectively, they were losing about 17 million Malaysian ringgit per year. We then had to decide whether to close some or all of these stores, and whether to close them gradually or at one shot. Shutting them down quickly meant taking some steep initial losses, since it involved breaking or negotiating our way out of leases, voluntary separation costs for staff, and all of the other issues involved in winding down a business.

I pushed the team hard to consider closing all of these stores quickly to eliminate underperforming outlets. Store closings are always a tricky time for company morale.

Cutting staff is never easy. Telling someone they no longer have a role is the toughest aspect of leadership and I never know how people will react. Some cry, some get angry. We chose to make this first cut the deepest so that we could then reassure people soon afterwards that we were growing again, rather than gradually chipping away at the company. In the end, we closed all 22 stores over the subsequent eight weeks.

The upshot was that we had pared back Courts Malaysia to the 50 best stores. We then engaged our supplier base to help us renovate and refurbish them. Many stores were still set up with an emphasis on furniture, so we wanted to reconfigure them to lead with electronics first to bring them in line with what had been working so well for us in Singapore. A lot of stores still displayed products by brand rather than by category, even though in Singapore we'd established years earlier that category management was able to produce far better results. As part of the renovation and refurbishing process, we also wanted to introduce the new Courts Singapore logo across both businesses and align the branding efforts, so we gave the stores a fresh look with new signage, new fixtures and so on.

We also put Courts Malaysia's marketing efforts and margins under the microscope. To my mind, Courts

Malaysia had been engaging in years of unnecessary marketing and promotion around interest rates and giving away freebies. For example, they had a lot of credit promotions such as if you bought a new TV, you'd get a half-price discount on another item. These sorts of deals were hurting the Malaysian business' margins, which were already low. It didn't help that they'd also pulled out of IT during the period of Courts Plc's administration, ostensibly due to low margins.

We decided to eliminate a lot of margin-eroding marketing campaigns, put in place a more sensible credit-marketing regime, re-introduce an IT range, and renew our focus on collecting debts and improving our bad-debt ratios. We also worked with our suppliers to align the trading terms in both Malaysia and Singapore.

Hindsight is nice, but it doesn't change what happened.

Meanwhile, we also discovered that in Malaysia we weren't getting the margins and rebate structures, or the advertising and in-store support that we were getting in Singapore. We quickly identified plenty of synergies that were relatively easy to implement in Malaysia since they were all things that we had already been doing in Singapore.

Over the subsequent year, we reduced our headcount in Malaysia from about 2,000 to 1,200 people. This included substantial cuts in layers of management that had built up within Courts Malaysia over the years as people were shuffled around to new jobs or kept on in roles that were not having a meaningful impact. Regardless of why they were kept on—perhaps the management in Malaysia had been too soft to make tough decisions on job cuts—the reality was that a significant headcount reduction was necessary to streamline the business and improve its financial health.

While we approached the store closures and job cuts with some trepidation, I think we built it up in our own minds to be a bigger challenge than it actually was. Fortunately, we discovered that when we put a voluntary separation scheme in front of people who had been with the company for a number of years, many of them were willing to leave and were very well rewarded for their decision. In the end, Courts Malaysia came out on the other side refreshed, realigned and ready for healthy growth.

GOODBYE THAILAND, FAREWELL INDONESIA
Meanwhile, after a bit of soul searching, I decided that we were going to get out of Thailand completely. We'd already started scaling back our business, but the remaining stores were still experiencing problems with creditors. I won't deny

that that was a painful decision for me, not to mention that it cost us around $30 million. If I were looking at a market entry today, I would go about it very differently, focusing on risk mitigation and partnership structures. Of course, hindsight is nice, but it doesn't change what happened. Our departure from Thailand in 2007 galvanised my desire to merge the Singapore and Malaysia businesses. It was almost like a mental scorecard for me: I wanted to make up the money we lost in Thailand by merging with and improving the business in Malaysia.

Following these final store closures we left a credit team in place in Thailand for another two and a half years or so to continue collecting on our existing credit book. Thanks to the efforts of our Thai finance director, Worranuch, and her team, we were fortunate that our bad experience in Thailand at least ended on a positive note. This team did an outstanding job and ended up collecting a higher proportion of our outstanding debts than we'd expected.

On another front, we met with banks in Malaysia and Indonesia to discuss Courts' business in Indonesia. A subsidiary of Courts Malaysia at the time, Courts Indonesia operated a network of 46 stores across the country, including one in the resort town of Lombok and a head office in Bali. It had undertaken a massive expansion programme across Java under previous management. When I came into the picture as deputy chairman of Courts Malaysia, the stores in Bali and Lombok were profitable but every single store in Java was making a loss. One of the key problems was that the Indonesia business hadn't grown its credit business fast enough to keep pace with store expansions.

Against this backdrop, it's no surprise that the Malaysian banks were unhappy that Courts Malaysia had bought a large stake in Courts Indonesia from the previous Indonesia partner, Matahari. And the Indonesian banks were disappointed that a small, profitable business in Bali and Lombok had become a loss-making business through a poorly planned expansion in Java. So the banks were unwilling to provide any further funding for the business, and I wasn't even going to try to get our shareholders to put new money into Indonesia—this would simply have been throwing good money after bad.

It then came down to a question of whether we could afford to simply pare back Courts Indonesia to just the profitable Bali and Lombok stores and continue to operate the business through internal funding, or whether we should pull the plug on the entire operation. Over time, we realised that trying to keep the business going—even a slimmed down version of it—wasn't going to work, so we stopped granting any new credit in Indonesia and started the process of winding down operations.

Unlike in Malaysia, we took a more gradual approach to winding down the business. The reason for this is that it cost us cash every time we closed a store. For instance, there were often penalties to be paid for breaking leases, and severance payments to be paid to employees who lost their jobs. Therefore, by paring back our stores slowly, we were able to use the inflow of cash from our existing Indonesian credit book to cover the costs and gradually pay down our bank debt. Another difference was that in Malaysia it was important to move swiftly so that we could start growing again as soon as possible, whereas in Indonesia the plan from the start was to shut down the entire operation, not to restart growth.

Starting from 46 stores, we gradually closed locations across Java—keeping a few of them open longer as collection centres for payments on our existing credit book—and within three years we made a complete exit, including the closure of the best performing stores in Lombok and Bali.

We were fortunate to have a director named Marwan Hanif to manage the process. Marwan joined us from

Wal-Mart. He'd worked in India and several other markets, and so he brought with him plenty of professional retail experience. At the time we were somewhat surprised that he took the country director position even though we'd told him when he joined that it was 90 per cent certain that his job would be to close down the company. Many people wouldn't be very keen to take on a role like that given that you'd basically be working yourself out of a job. However, Marwan is an Indonesian and he was keen to get back into the Indonesian market after having spent several years abroad. I guess he viewed this as an opportunity that would help him re-enter the local retail scene, and by keeping him on, Courts could keep a presence in Indonesia, too.

By spreading the process over three years, we were able to pay all of our suppliers, staff and banks in full. While I'm a big fan of the Indonesian market, it didn't make sense at the time to try to keep that incarnation of Courts Indonesia business alive.

TOUGH DECISIONS FOR A BRIGHTER FUTURE
Making these changes in Malaysia, Thailand and Indonesia involved tough decisions—stores were closed, jobs were cut and businesses were shut down. As a business leader, you

generally don't want to see your business shrinking or being permanently laid to rest. When your goal is to expand a company and achieve top-line and bottom-line growth, such moves can feel like a step in the wrong direction. Even worse, they can feel like an admission of failure and proof that somewhere earlier on wrong decisions were made.

However, in business it is important to recognise that sometimes long-term growth requires short-term cuts and rationalisation. And more importantly, having the courage and objectivity to make the tough decisions is far better than being hampered in your decision-making by pride or regret. So while I wish that the cuts and closures that we implemented hadn't been necessary, I was heartened by the thought that our actions now would help us become stronger and smarter in the future.

CHAPTER 11
Full Steam Ahead

There's a time for turnaround and there's a time for growth, and each period requires a different approach. When turning a business around, the management focuses on making tough decisions, having compassionate conversations and maintaining a low profile. Once the house is in order, it's all about aggressively driving sales and raising the brand profile. The same process can be applied to one's career.

HITTING A WALL AND CLIMBING OVER

Once Courts merged its Singapore and Malaysia businesses, we began seeing positive results from Malaysia—though they didn't translate into an immediate boost in profits. At the start of this period the combined Singapore and Malaysia businesses were more or less breaking even. In the following financial year, 2008/2009, we made a combined profit of about $3.5 million.

This relatively modest profit was not really reflective of how well things were progressing at this time. We had taken some large one-off costs associated with restructuring following the acquisition by Baring. We'd also taken a hit from the financial crisis that hit markets worldwide in 2008. Strong results during the first half of the 2008 financial year came to a sudden halt in October. We had been planning to securitise our Malaysian consumer finance assets and had already amortised existing debt, but as the markets dried up, we found ourselves in a tight position for a few months.

While disheartening, we certainly didn't let the situation discourage us from pressing ahead with our strategy. Instead, we responded rapidly and decisively to minimise the negative impact of the crisis. Internally, we trimmed costs in various parts of the business. All staff took slight pay cuts and extended working hours, and expatriate members of our management team gave up their housing and maid allowances and other benefits. In return, we implemented a performance-based bonus scheme that rewarded employees based on economic value added. I also made a commitment to everyone in the organisation that there would be no other layoffs, and I am proud of the fact that we stuck to this.

We also renegotiated all of our marketing contracts in both Singapore and Malaysia. For example, we negotiated a deal with our media partners whereby they would be responsible for some of the back-end work related to our marketing efforts. TV stations helped with the production of our TV ad campaigns; newspaper companies took up some of the print costs and waived positioning fees related to our print ads; and our printer took on some marketing-related photography work. We were all in the same boat, and we were all looking to stay afloat. These changes led to major savings in our marketing budget, which in turn created a bit of an internal marketing war chest. By shifting a lot of our spending from the back-end to the front-end, we saw a 20 to 30 per cent boost in our marketing firepower during this period.

LESSON

And I learned a valuable lesson: **Negotiate— or renegotiate—everything.** Having good negotiation skills can benefit both individuals and organisations. But these skills won't do you much good if you don't use them. For instance, if your company has a five-year lease on a property, this doesn't mean you can't go back to the owner and ask to renegotiate before the lease is up. Just because your company has had a 40-hour work week for decades doesn't mean you can't negotiate with your staff to shift to a 44 hour work week. The same principle applies to individuals negotiating their employment terms. The key is to realise that everything is negotiable.

Another important development during that period was the launch of our Courts Price Promise at the start of 2009. This was right in the thick of the financial crisis, and during this period we reorganised our marketing to focus on offering value. We decided to apply as much of our marketing budget as possible towards keeping prices low. Any resources that might previously have gone into promotions such as lucky draws or win-a-car competitions were instead directed to price discounts. We also decided that if we were going to give away free gifts with purchases, they would be directly tied to the purchase. For example, if you bought a television you might receive a free DVD player; the purchase of a bed would include free pillows. We also implemented a proactive competitive pricing system based on daily checks of our competitors' prices.

Although the crisis hit hard, we managed to recover quite quickly. In October, November and December 2008 we saw sales fall by double-digit percentages, followed by a drop of about three per cent in January and February 2009. However, by March 2009—thanks to our improved marketing firepower—we were back into positive revenue growth as sales picked up quite nicely and got us off to a great start for the 2009/2010 financial year. Sales also received a boost thanks to the stimulus packages introduced by the governments in Singapore and Malaysia.

Be underpaid and over-deliver.

Besides these results, one unexpected bonus of our recovery strategy was receiving an International Management Action Award in 2010 by the Chartered Management Institute (Singapore) in recognition for our swift and effective response to the global financial crisis. In the same year, I received the title as an Officer of the Most Excellent Order of the British Empire (OBE) by Her Majesty The Queen, in recognition of my role promoting UK business interests for the British Chamber of Commerce. I also received a Lifetime Achievement Award from the Institute of Advertising in Singapore (IAS) the same year. All these things happened in such a short time span, and with no change of context, personal or professional, for me. So I guess we were doing something right.

LESSON

Just to be clear, though, I have never chased rewards, I have chased effectiveness. And in that spirit, I offer another lesson: **Be underpaid and over-deliver on your responsibilities.** No matter how good your work is, you're not an asset unless you're nearly underpaid. Your boss will not want to promote you—or perhaps even keep you around—if you are being paid more than the value that you bring to the company. On the other hand, delivering results beyond your pay grade will keep you in demand—and may earn you a few trophies along the way.

In Malaysia, the closing of stores in the previous year and the continued execution of the Bain plan meant that Courts Malaysia went from a more or less break-even position in 2008/2009 to making a profit of 13 million Malaysian ringgit in 2009/2010. Courts Singapore's profit also grew during this period, resulting in a five-fold increase in the overall profitability of Courts Asia.

As the economy began picking up, we began opening more stores in Malaysia. By mid 2010, we had aligned the Malaysia business with the Courts branding being used in Singapore. We had also refurbished all of Malaysian stores to lead with consumer electronics rather than furniture. This change was much easier following the severing of ties with the UK, since Courts Singapore no longer carried the emotional baggage of Courts' furniture-first heritage. We didn't consider furniture unimportant, we were simply acknowledging the reality that electronics is a sexier product category to have in the windows to draw customers inside. Sofas and beds are typically not impulse buys, after all.

The result of all of these factors was a tripling of profit in Malaysia to about 36 million Malaysian ringgit. Our business in Singapore also continued to flourish and saw an increase in profit of about 50 per cent. Overall, Courts Asia's profit roughly doubled in 2010/2011, placing us far ahead of all of our competitors in Southeast Asia.

UNFETTERED

Over the first few years post-acquisition, we built a better business with a strong brand identity, clear corporate objectives and robust financial performance, even without having a head office to answer to. Our private equity shareholders were more concerned with value creation than with immediate results, so we could focus solely on the parts of the business that would produce long-term results. However, I don't think we would have achieved anywhere close to this level of success without the team of managers that we had in place, a team that together produced a new vision for Courts. If I thought of the Ged-ites as a culture within Courts traditional culture, my new team was a culture that had grown organically outside of this culture

Since James Friel and his team had done an excellent job steadying the ship in Malaysia, I asked James back to Singapore to take on the role of regional commercial director and later promoted him to chief operating officer. Meanwhile, Chris Yong—whom James had recruited two years earlier from Microsoft—took over as country director for Malaysia, a position he held until 2012. Chan Yuen Keong, the credit director whom James had hired to clean up the credit book in Malaysia, was subsequently promoted to the position of regional credit director.

In Singapore, Kee Kim Eng was promoted from Singapore finance director to chief financial officer for Courts Asia. Other key members of the Singapore management team also remained with the business, such as Steve Church, who is now our category director for furniture (regional) and merchandise director (Singapore), and Kiran Kaur, who continues to do an excellent job as our regional HR director.

The team during this period combined managers with extensive experience in Singapore with individuals well-versed in some of the new challenges that we were facing, such as creating data diagnostics to evaluate credit lines. I believe that our team has been so effective because it was united by a mutual interest in serving the company, which was one of the principal messages that I brought away from working with Neville.

> **I've noticed a few managers over the years at Courts who have struggled to 'fit in' because they were unaccustomed to my apolitical approach.**

Since 1998, when I became deputy-managing director of Courts Singapore, I have done my best to create an apolitical environment. I have always valued an egalitarian workplace, but I think my views on this were hardened by my experience at Colorvision when Neville brought in Alan Tinger as managing director, who tolerated an atmosphere of company politicking and hierarchies. Ironically, I've noticed a few managers over the years at Courts who have struggled to 'fit in' because they were unaccustomed to my apolitical approach.

I believe that building and maintaining a strong team requires a degree of flexibility on both sides—particularly in a company such as Courts, that blends eastern and western cultures. There is a constant effort to solve company problems, and that helps to lessen tendencies for corporate clique formation. Sometimes we ask people to carry a bit of additional responsibility if we're in the process of juggling our resources and shifting staff around to fill different roles. Other times it's the company that needs to be flexible in accommodating the personal and family needs of our team members. In the end, it is all about having the company's best interests at heart and striving for a common goal.

TIME TO LIST?

Baring's acquisition in 2007 played a critical role in enabling us to transform Courts' operations in Asia for the better. At the same time, the acquisition terms and ownership structure placed some constraints on our ability to operate freely, such as by dictating how our profits could be used.

Keen to be masters of our own destiny, we felt that tapping into public funds via an initial public offering (IPO) would enable us to both accelerate our growth and achieve greater freedom to determine the direction of the company.

We filed a draft prospectus with the Monetary Authority of Singapore in March 2010, and then began pitching our IPO to institutional investors in Singapore and Hong Kong with three appointed advisors—Macquarie Capital Asia, RBS Group and CLSA Asia-Pacific Markets. Unfortunately, the demand was lukewarm.

A key challenge was the fact that markets worldwide were still reeling from the financial slowdown that began in 2008. With the US and European economies still struggling along, the market for IPOs was relatively weak and valuations were under pressure. The IPOs that were taking place at the time were being done at prices that reflected very low price/earnings multiples, or they were offering very high dividends. Either way, these were not ideal circumstances.

2010 marked a 'lightbulb' moment for me. I was disappointed that Courts did not list.

Could we have gotten the IPO over the line in 2010? Maybe. But all signs suggested that conditions weren't ripe. The amount we could have raised by listing would not have been sufficient to retire all of our acquisition financing, provide us with funds to grow *and* give shareholders an acceptable return. Therefore, in June 2010 we decided to put our public listing plans on hold.

At the same time, I felt a sense of urgency to take Courts' business to a new level and set ambitious performance targets. This was not the end of our IPO ambitions. But it was a time to shift gears and pursue another corporate development plan.

CHAPTER 12
Blueprint 2.0

Setting an ultra-ambitious target can frustrate teams, or galvanise them. I believe that the difference lies in how target—and its purpose—is framed.

Those who know me would probably agree that I'm not the type to sit quietly in one spot for too long. I suppose this is because I feel energised when I'm active. Since it's not in my nature to take my foot off the gas, it should come as no surprise that my team and I had (and still have) plenty of big plans for taking Courts Asia forward in the years ahead. While it was certainly a disappointment that our IPO efforts in 2010 didn't get off the ground, this did not deter us from pushing ahead with a variety of bold initiatives aimed at driving growth—a strategy that is still very much central to Courts' business.

Going through the company's financials, I saw that we had a three-year track record of delivery, but since two of those three years were turnaround, maybe we didn't have the track record needed. So this realisation gave us the heightened sense of urgency and drive to really boost our results over the next couple of years to ensure that when and if we went to list again, we would succeed.

By early 2011, plans started to take shape in what Bain named 'Blueprint 2.0'—a multi-pronged strategy for growth. It's still ongoing, but Blueprint 2.0 has centred on a few core elements, which I describe below.

1. IMPROVING EXISTING STORE PERFORMANCE

Growing our business means opening new stores, but we can also reap improvements in sales performance by enhancing our existing stores, for example, by optimising the merchandise mix, space allocation and product placement within our stores.

Blueprint 2.0 has involved accelerating our refurbishment programme for existing stores in both Singapore and Malaysia. For example, in 2012, we remodelled our Megastore in Tampines for the first time since it opened in 2006. We made a lot of changes, such as adding more multi-channel features around the store. Shoppers can now take advantage of internet kiosks and many more service points. Some of the changes were based on ideas gathered during recent international study trips, which we were excited to introduce to the Singapore market.

Other store developments have been tied to specific suppliers. For example, we are in the process of rolling out 28 Apple store-in-store concepts in Malaysia, which we expect to give a healthy boost to our sale of Apple products.

Another major development for us is an agreement with Singapore's three big telcos—M1, SingTel and Starhub—to set up in our stores. This was a major coup for us, as we became the first retailer in Singapore to convince the telcos to compete under the same roof.

To do this, we went in to talk with the CEO of each telco with a sales pitch to sell the services of all three companies through the same retail network (Courts, naturally).

I highlighted the challenge faced by each company in maintaining its presence across Singapore via an expensive network of retail outlets given the limits on economies of scale when individual retailers can work with only one telco. Wouldn't it be more efficient to take advantage of our existing—and growing—network of stores across the island? Why not at least try it out as a pilot project?

Initially, there were doubts—both from within my own team and from the middle management at the telcos—with people saying that there's no way the companies will ever agree to this. The inevitable question was raised: if all three telcos are in the same store, how will you decide whose services to sell? But that is exactly the same situation Courts confronts with its electrical, IT and furniture products. We will set sales targets and then work towards reaching those targets. If one telco's plan is no better or worse than its competitors' plans, we remain market neutral.

Despite the early doubts, my discussions with each of the CEOs went very well and all three said 'alright, let's give this a try'. It's still early days for this initiative, so I do not yet have any results to share, but I can say that I believe we've made another Courts-led breakthrough in Singapore's retail space.

2. GROWING OUR LAND-BASED FOOTPRINT

Going forward, we intend to expand Courts' footprint, aiming to add an average of six stores per year in Malaysia and one store per year in Singapore over the next two to three years. For example, in Singapore, we entered into a lease for a new store in JEM, a new retail mall in the Jurong district, helping to boost our presence in the western part of Singapore. We also see potential to open new Courts in some of Singapore's underserved locations.

I see considerable potential to further build our position in Malaysia—up to as many as 95 stores, given that the market for electrical and IT products remains fragmented.

Of course, it was only a few years ago that we exited both Thailand and Indonesia. I have certainly not forgotten our missteps there. Indeed, the problems that we faced in those two markets sit clearly in my mind whenever considering further expansion. At the same time, I don't believe in giving up on expansion simply because things didn't pan out an earlier attempt.

With this in mind, we are moving forward with plans to re-enter Indonesia, which has just grown more attractive as the economy grows. This time though, instead of the small stores Courts had in Bali, Lombok and scattered across Java, we are starting out in Jakarta with a Megastore format, which allows us both to bypass rising shopping mall rents and benefit from economies of scale, not to mention offering consumers free parking, food and beverage outlets, and kids' spaces.

3. EXPLOITING NEW CHANNELS
In the online realm, we re-launched eCourts, our online store, in October 2012. In keeping with the growth of ecommerce globally, our new site offers double the number of stock-keeping units (SKUs) previously available.

It also boasts features such as 'Cash on Delivery' and 'Click & Collect'. Cash on Delivery allows customers to shop online but pay in cash when their purchases are delivered, thus avoiding entering credit card details online. Alternatively, Click & Collect enables customers to shop and pay online, but to collect purchases in person, thus avoiding the cost of delivery.

Body doubles, zip-lines and heart attacks

The re-launch of eCourts provided an opportunity for a bit of fun. In the past, we'd open new Courts stores with traditional ribbon-cutting ceremonies.

In keeping with the times, our marketing team suggested that consumers determine how to celebrate the eCourts opening by voting on Facebook, where we have about 74,000 fans. The choices were: doing the reverse bungee jump at Clarke Quay, doing a tightrope walk or doing the Megazip flying fox at Sentosa.

It would be an understatement to say that my wife was not keen on any of these plans. Although I had recently been given a clean bill of health, Janice contacted our doctor to ask him to warn me against participating of these activities. She went so far as to make arrangements for a body double to do the actual stunt for me.

A body double is not my style, so after the flying fox scored the most votes on Facebook, our team showed up at Megazip on Sentosa, Singapore's resort island, to mark the estore opening. After harnessing up, docking a

Terry after the Megazip.

helmet-mounted camera, and grabbing a pair of scissors, I zipped across the jungle canopy. A bright yellow Courts ribbon had been slung between two cables near the end of the zip line, and just as I went soaring past at 60km per hour, I snipped the ribbon. To be honest, it was harder than I had expected, but I did hit my target!

4. INNOVATING CREDIT SERVICES

Credit services have been an integral part of Courts' successful business model, but a changing market landscape led us to roll out two new credit products in Singapore aimed to serve the diversifying needs and preferences of our customers. For example, our 'S & E Pass Flexi Plan' allows foreign workers and expatriates with an S Pass or Employment Pass—two different types of employment visa issued by the Singapore government—to purchase on credit. These groups typically do not have access to credit facilities in Singapore through financial institutions or other types of creditors, in part because they were seen as high risk.

SmartRent is another option enabling customers to rent products instead of purchasing them. Although Singaporeans are also eligible, we designed SmartRent primarily with expatriates in mind.

Going against the grain, as Courts is known to do, we determined that with the right criteria and the right contract length, together with a bit more stringency on our part, we could service these groups and in doing so, open up a whole new market.

CHAPTER 13
Going Public

At some point in your career, you'll feel planted on firm ground. This is not a time for hubris, but a time to be self-assured about expected outcomes.

The implementation of Blueprint 2.0 helped Courts to achieve a banner year in FY 2011, with net profit of $32 million on total sales of $674 million. In FY 2012 these figures jumped to $39 million net profit on $724 million in total sales. These results represented compound annual growth rates of 11.8 per cent in total sales and 47.4 per cent in net profit from 2010—strong by any measure.

While all this was happening, between 2010 and 2012, we met with several strategic investors who expressed interest in possibly acquiring Courts Asia. We also continued to look at the possibility of a public listing, and kept in close touch with bankers at UOB Kay Hian, a Singapore-based brokerage. I had mixed feelings regarding these two options. If forced to choose between going public or selling the business to a strategic investor lacking the right fit, I would have preferred to go public, because I felt that the option would give us more flexibility going forward. But if the right strategic investor had come along—such as a multinational conglomerate with people who understood and complemented our business model—this option could have proven attractive. Such an investor might have offered access to extensive financial resources, as well as opportunities to develop new business strategies. But it was stressful, always being in the shop window.

Fortunately, some factors were converging to help steer our course. Perhaps critically, by early 2012, market conditions had improved. And Courts was running strong. Personally, I had also made strides. While I had stepped down from my Presidency at the British

Chamber, I'd become much more active in the Young Presidents Organisation, a group connecting over 20,000 'young' (under 45 years old) CEOs worldwide to share ideas and leadership practices. I served as YPO's Regional Communications Chairperson. And sticking to what I know best, I led marketing and sales for the YPO Global Leadership Conference in Singapore in 2012, held at the Marina Bay Sands Hotel.

By joining YPO, I was not only exercising my skills, I was learning from other high energy CEOs of bigger companies, which I found both energising and challenging. I've integrated some of my experiences with YPO into my own management style, such as celebrating successes with colleagues. For instance, after our team had delivered such outstanding results in 2011 and 2012, I asked our shareholders for permission to spend a few hundred thousand dollars taking them on a first-class trip to Shanghai. We worked and we celebrated. And I thanked each team member by delivering personalised, hand-written notes to their rooms every night.

LESSON

Celebrate success with your team, your family and alone. Most of the time, success comes only after tremendous effort, hard work and perseverance, so it is important to take the time to acknowledge and enjoy your achievements when they come. For a management team, the truly motivational moments are when you celebrate together and galvanise your ongoing commitment to take things to the next level. Celebrating with family is also important as a way of reminding them that they are important to you and part of your life and success. Career success often requires sacrifices and compromises at home, so support from your family is a key contributor to your achievements at work. Lastly, remember to celebrate in private, however you like to do that. Take a day off, enjoy a fine scotch or simply pause to raise your hat to a job well done.

....

THE RIGHT TEAM FOR THE JOB

By mid-2102, due to a combination of improving market conditions and Courts' strong performance in 2012, our Board grew convinced that we should make another IPO attempt. We brought HSBC on board as advisors, and as the sole global coordinator, bookrunner, underwriter and issue manager for the listing. UOB Kay Hian served as the public offer coordinator and sub-placement agent.

Our second attempt at IPO proved to be a completely different experience. For example, HSBC was introducing us to potential investors who were asking well-informed, retail savvy questions about like-for-like sales, sales per square foot, etc. Our IPO 'sales' team—me, Kee Kim Eng (our CFO) and Chan Yuen Keong (our regional credit director), together with the bankers from HSBC—demonstrated great team energy. I would start by running through a presentation about our business from a strategic and commercial perspective. Yuen Keong would then step up to give more specifics on how he and his team turned around Courts' credit portfolio and why this is sustainable for the future. And Kim would talk about our series of securitisations and how our capital structure is well aligned to our business. Our presentation was seamless thanks to our many years of collaboration, and as a team we were clearly well prepared and in sync with each other. During one meeting with a potential investor, when asked where to find a particular piece of information in the prospectus, all three of us—Kim, Yuen Keong and I—said at the same time, "It's on page 32."

In fact, it was so smooth that I often presented without notes—something that took our HSBC bankers by surprise.

Nor did we receive—or need—any coaching this time. Nevertheless, throughout this process we received positive feedback via HSBC from all of the investors we met.

All this is not to say that we proceeded without some hiccups. For instance, I remember that in Hong Kong, we faced a particularly tough grilling. But by 2012, I really didn't let it affect me whether or not a particular investor decided to invest. This wasn't arrogance—it was simply borne out of my belief that we have a great story and great prospects. It was about deciding to approach things in a different style and having a greater understanding of what was going to work with the people we were meeting. I answered investors' questions with the information that I felt most relevant, not with answers that I thought they expected. In the end, it seems to have worked.

We went on the road with HSBC as part of the book-building process, spending two days in Singapore, two days in Hong Kong, and a day and a half in London. Our discussions with institutional investors in Singapore went smoothly since our brand is well known and we'd been through the process before. In Hong Kong, we had to step up our game because investors there were less familiar with our brand and seemed to be more sceptical. Some of the investors there were really sharp, but HSBC did a good job of briefing us about each one, including their profile and what to expect.

Ironically, in London, Courts' original market, the reception was mixed. We spoke with two hedge funds there that had done their homework and knew exactly what information they wanted from us. However, we also met with a couple of investors who were completely out-to-lunch with a narrow 'Middle England' frame of reference and absolutely no understanding of the market situation in Asia. They also had poor opinions of the electronics retail business in general, since the business wasn't faring well in the UK.

A BETTER APPROACH

A key difference in our approach to the IPO in 2012 is that we started with a cornerstone process. If you are unfamiliar with this term—as I was prior to embarking upon the IPO process—it refers to investors who publicly commit to making a large, predetermined investment in the IPO before it is officially launched. This process helps to lend credibility to the IPO and stimulate demand amongst other investors. (In contrast, our IPO attempt in 2010 began straight with a book-building process, without any cornerstone investors. In hindsight, I can see that this put us at a disadvantage, especially when trying to drum up interest amongst institutional investors outside of Singapore as some of them were unfamiliar with Courts.)

With HSBC's help, we pitched a number of potential cornerstone investors and ended up signing on four well-known and respected institutions: JF Asset Management, New Silk Road Investment, Target Asset Management and Value Partners Hong Kong. Each agreed to take a $15 million stake in our IPO. In addition, unlike in 2010, Kim and I also committed $15 million each, which gave us a great boost when we subsequently went on the road to pitch the IPO to other institutional investors by demonstrating our commitment to Courts.

My financial commitment to Courts' public listing demonstrates another contrast with our previous IPO attempt. Remember that I'm a retail expert, not a banker. In 2010—my first time pitching to investors as part of a book-building process—I wasn't sure how best to manage the situation. I approached the process with the attitude that I was the retail expert and the investor was the investment expert, and therefore the kinds of questions they asked were the only ones that mattered. I think at the time I felt somewhat like a rookie, unable to exercise the kind of flair that I did in other aspects of my life.

At the end of the whole process our institutional book was 3.4 times subscribed and our retail book was 24.4 times subscribed. These figures reflected strong interest in our IPO, and sealed the deal for our listing. So at 8:58am on Monday, 15 October 2012, Courts went public.

LISTED!

With an IPO offering price of $0.77 for our 178 million ordinary shares—raising gross proceeds of $137 million—Courts Asia debuted on the SGX Mainboard at $0.81. It was quite a thrill to see our brand new stock symbol on the screen as trading got underway. At the end of our first day of trading, Courts Asia closed at $0.785 after 34.9 million shares changed hands, making us the day's fourth most active stock.

Of course, the IPO is hardly the end of our story. It has simply brought us to the end of one chapter and launched us firmly into the next. I am extremely happy with the outcome of the entire IPO process, and I am of course proud of our team.

Courts is now turning its full attention back to the art of retailing. Now that we have been remade in Asia—both Courts and I—there is so much that we hope to achieve in the years ahead, and as usual I am brimming with energy to get rolling!

CHAPTER 14
Thinking Big[ger]

The IPO, the year 2013, and the publication of this book, mark two decades of my work with Courts. I almost wanted to call this book 'Lessons at Half-Time', in reference to my love for football *and* in recognition that my career path, and the lessons it's taught me along the way, is nowhere near complete. I also considered not titling the book at all—not publishing it. There were times—there are still times—when the idea of publishing a memoir seems, well, a bit vulgar, or at least self-indulgent. After all, who writes a memoir at the age of 44?

My answer, of course, is 'Who says I shouldn't? Why not?' I've proven repeatedly that I can achieve the unexpected when I set my mind to it. I set myself a target deadline; I found a team to help me; and I devoted time to the goal.

The question is, why? Why write a book? Why lead Courts to IPO? Why dress like a geisha and dance on stage? Why give to charity? Why look for mentors? Why *become* a mentor? I am tempted to say, flippantly, 'why not'? But that would overlook some of the critical forces of my—and, I would argue, anyone's success: thinking big, working towards a greater good, *becoming* that greater good, and serving the greater good.

To mark my 20 years with Courts, and to close the book, I want to elaborate on some of these key drivers that have helped me achieve my professional and personal ambitions. I've strung several learning points throughout this book. The ones that follow are broader in application, and are meant to guide any kind of reader—professional or not—in their pursuits.

Key to all of my observations is the core belief that thinking 'big' is a critical platform for success. However, having big ideas and dreams is only the first step in the journey—achieving them requires a whole lot of hard work, perseverance, a bit of luck, and an ability to ask, 'why not?'

1. **THINK BIG, THINK IMPRACTICALLY, THEN MAKE IT REAL**

   What excites you? What do you dream of doing? What do you hope to accomplish personally or professionally? Thinking big allows you to expand your view of what's possible and set your sights on the things that you would most like to achieve. From there, you can take a step back to do a realistic assessment of what it will take to reach your goals, or at least reach an approximation of your goals.

2. **ALWAYS HAVE A MENTOR**

   Mentors can greatly accelerate your learning and enable you to advance in your career in ways that would be difficult to achieve on your own. While mentors can play an invaluable role in your development, it is also important to recognise that they will not be with you forever. Instead, you need to find individuals who are a good fit for you and reflect your growth at different stages in your career. Looking back on my career thus far, mentors such as Neville Michaelson, Bryan Brooks and Leo McKee each played crucial yet very different roles in helping me reach where I am today.

3. **USE PAST HARDSHIP AS A STRENGTH, NOT A CROSS TO BEAR**

   There were some points in my childhood that were particularly rocky, although I certainly realise that millions of children have faced far more difficult circumstances than I did. Whatever the hardships you have faced in the past, the key is to use them to make yourself stronger, rather than as an excuse to fail. Coming from a relatively poor background made me hungry to achieve and taught me that no one was going to serve me on a silver platter.

4. **DON'T ALLOW YOUR RELATIONSHIP WITH AN AUTHORITY FIGURE TO HOLD YOU BACK**

   Whatever your circumstances, your relationship with your boss, or whatever authority you answer to can be an excellent opportunity for professional and personal development—whether it's picking up skills and knowledge from a great boss who mentors you, or simply learning how to effectively manage a difficult person.

5. **BE MENTALLY PREPARED TO BE FIRED OR REJECTED FOR DOING THE RIGHT THING**

   I feel that I've been at my best professionally when I felt completely free from the fear of dismissal. This goes hand in hand with having self-confidence and believing that your behaviour and values are aligned with what is right. If you have a good reputation and relationships in the industry, then finding another job if necessary shouldn't be too difficult. There is no shame in being asked to leave by an employer who's made a mistake. Having the courage to stick to your principles is a positive managerial quality.

6. **STAY GROUNDED**

   As you rise higher within an organisation your perspective of the business will change, but don't get stuck with your head in the clouds. Can you still have a real conversation with staff at all levels, whether in the warehouse or on the shop floor? The best leaders are able to thrive with increasingly greater responsibilities and, at the same time, connect in meaningful ways with everyone in the company.

   For instance, at Courts we have long implemented monthly breakfasts with new recruits, lunches with middle managers in groups of eight to 12, skip level one to one discussions, staff appreciation trees, a hall of fame awards, and management serving staff at the annual company dinner and dance.

These programmes are managed by our HR team but fronted by myself and senior leaders. Walk the talk is a cliché but you're either present, engaged, visible and aligned with the teaming behaviours that you're asking others to exhibit—or you're not.

7. **PLAY**

It's so important to play together. Social media, and Facebook in particular, has made me realise how precious that photo with the staff at the company function, celebration of a win or department gathering, can be. Team players need role models and the more accessible, relaxed, down to earth and maybe even offbeat, you are, the more others relax around you and the more real bonding, communication, dialogue and, ultimately, loyalty will occur. People don't leave companies—they leave bosses. And shared successes, memories and happy times are tough to exit.

About the Author

TERRY O'CONNOR is the Chief Executive Officer (CEO) of Courts Asia, one of Asia's leading electrical, IT and furniture retailers.

Hailing from Liverpool, England, Terry started his career in retailing in the cut-throat UK electrical retail marketplace with Colorvision PLC, rising to the post of Buying Director at the age of 23. In 1993, Terry was hired by Courts to spearhead its acceleration into the electrical retail market in Singapore, holding the posts of Buying Director from 1993 to 1997, Commercial Director from 1997 to 1998 and Deputy Managing Director from 1998 to 2000 before assuming the role of Managing Director in 2000. After the private equity-led buyout of Courts operations in Southeast Asia in 2007, Terry assumed the role of CEO for Courts in Asia and has since led a turnaround of its operations in Malaysia.

Terry is also a leading figure in the wider British community in Singapore. He was the President of the British Chamber of Commerce (BritCham) from 2006 to 2010 and the President of the British Club from 1999 to 2002. Under his leadership at the BritCham, it grew to become an active organisation with over 1,000 members, delivering valuable services to the British business community in Singapore. Terry has also spearheaded links with other British Chambers in neighbouring countries to identify synergies and opportunities in Southeast Asia.

Additionally, Terry holds the post of President at the Institute of Advertising, Singapore and is also the Chapter Chair of Young Presidents' Organisation (YPO), which is a not-for-profit, global network of young chief executives connected around the shared mission of becoming 'Better Leaders through Education and Idea Exchange'. He was also recently appointed by the Minister of Education as a Member of the National Youth Achievement Award (NYAA) Advisory Board for a three-year-term from 2013 to 2016.

An active member in public and community service, Terry is a regular commentator in both the local and regional media on retail issues. He and his wife have been actively involved in charitable activities and have helped raised funds for causes such as Down Syndrome, Breast Cancer, Cerebral Palsy, Red Cross Home for the Disabled and Riding for the Disabled.

Terry holds a Master of Business Administration in Retailing and Wholesaling from the University of Stirling. He is married to Janice and they have two lovely children.

Terry was conferred the award of Officer of the Most Excellent Order of the British Empire (OBE) by Her Majesty The Queen of England in June 2010.